LOCATION MAP

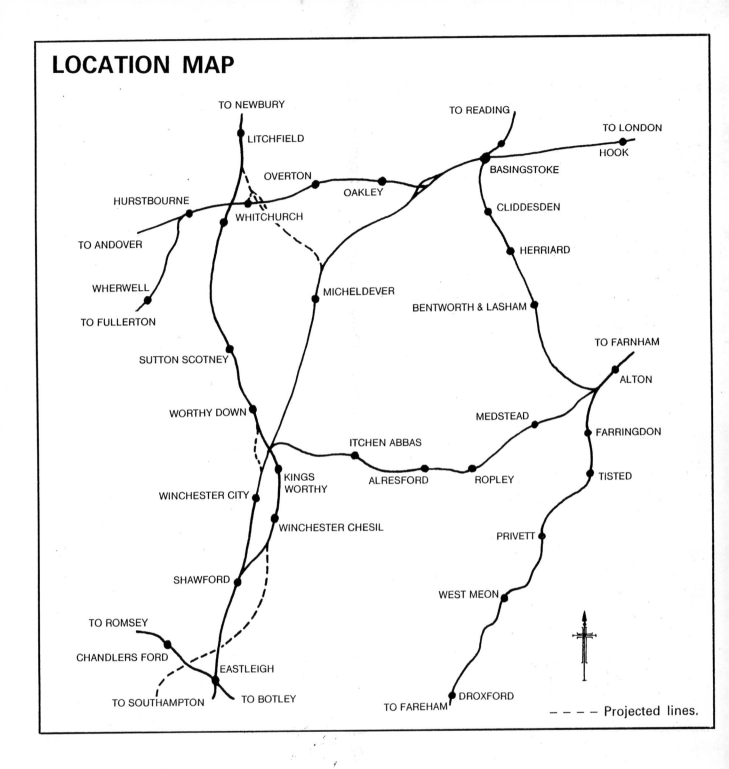

TO NEWBURY

TO READING

TO LONDON

LITCHFIELD

HOOK

OVERTON

BASINGSTOKE

OAKLEY

HURSTBOURNE

CLIDDESDEN

WHITCHURCH

TO ANDOVER

HERRIARD

WHERWELL

MICHELDEVER

TO FULLERTON

BENTWORTH & LASHAM

TO FARNHAM

SUTTON SCOTNEY

ALTON

WORTHY DOWN

MEDSTEAD

FARRINGDON

ITCHEN ABBAS

KINGS WORTHY

ALRESFORD

ROPLEY

TISTED

WINCHESTER CITY

WINCHESTER CHESIL

PRIVETT

SHAWFORD

WEST MEON

TO ROMSEY

CHANDLERS FORD

EASTLEIGH

TO SOUTHAMPTON

TO BOTLEY

DROXFORD

TO FAREHAM

– – – – Projected lines.

THE RAILWAYS OF WINCHESTER

KEVIN ROBERTSON
&
ROGER SIMMONDS

Published by Platform 5 Publishing Ltd., Lydgate House, Lydgate Lane, Sheffield S10 5FH.

Printed by Oxford University Press Printing House, Walton Street, Oxford.

ISBN 0 906579 71 6

Class H15 4–6–0 No. 30489 near Winchester in early BR days.

Donovan E.H. Box

CONTENTS

INTRODUCTION

It was with more than a little scepticism that I accepted the invitation to produce a book on the history of the railways of Winchester. Scepticism, because having lived in the area for most of my life I soon found I knew far less about my own local area than perhaps railways in other parts of the country. But nonetheless the research necessary has provided a fascinating insight into a part of local history I had failed to realise had even existed and so to all those who have so freely given their help I extend my sincere gratitude. Especially, at this stage, I thank my co-author Roger Simmonds, for when faced with a personal crisis he has found the time to prepare much in the way of the text whilst finding also numerous fascinating photographs.

The result then is what we hope will be a readable history of the lines extending to a five mile radius of Winchester and in this way encompass the main line from Wallers Ash as far as Otterbourne, the DN & S north to Worthy Down and the Alton line to Itchen Abbas. Special emphasis is however given to the South Western side for the DN & S is, we hope, well documented in our previously published works.

Possibly the hardest choice has been what to leave out and certainly not, as we perhaps first thought, what to put in. In consequence here is the ideal opportunity to utilise those many fascinating snippets that invariably turn up as a by-product of other research and which would otherwise be confined to the files, possibly never to see the light of day.

Today the DN & S and Alton lines are no more, their paths slowly reverting back to nature and with the passage of time the memories of the traveller becoming a little hazy. The aim of this book is to re-kindle a few of those memories.

Kevin Robertson

Eastleigh 1987

CHAPTER 1

THE SOUTH WESTERN

The City of Winchester

Arguably foremost amongst the towns of Hampshire, Winchester may rightly claim an ancestry dating back well before the compilation of the Domesday Book. In consequence, it has evolved with a mixture of ancient edifices; the Cathedral, College and Westgate to name but a few. Such great and well known attractions have in the past tended to cast shadows over less well known and seemingly less glamorous aspects of the City, often all the more interesting by the very fact that they do not attract such a plethora of visitors.

Strolling then through some of the quiet backstreets, one will find medieval dwelling houses and small alleyways, many reminiscent of York, although it must be said not in such quantity. But it is not only with regard to its buildings and monuments that the City may stake a claim to history, for the means of providing public transport to Winchester is itself a fascinating story and certainly one with a justifiable claim to attention in the same way as the monuments at the Buttercross and King Alfred's statue.

Apart from the coach roads and footpaths criss-crossing the county, the most well known of which must be the Pilgrims Way, public transport really began in 1710, the time the Itchen Navigation is believed to have opened for traffic. Thus there was now a means of transporting goods from Southampton to Winchester. The original intention of the promoters was to progress further and connect with the Basingstoke Canal and so provide for an alternative route to the capital avoiding the long sea passage around the south coast. For various reasons however this was never carried out and instead the navigation (the word referring to an improved river rather than a complete new waterway) found scant use, providing little prosperity to either the area or owning bursars.

Station Hill, Winchester. As the name suggests this leads to the 'City' station which is behind the photographer. Out of sight to the right is the South Western Hotel, named after the railway, whilst beyond is White & Co., the removal company, on the 'six way' junction with Swan Lane, City Road, Sussex Street, Stockbridge Road and Andover Road. *D.C. Dine.*

The Building of the Main Line

The benefits of a railway linking London with Southampton had been extolled from about 1831 onwards, several clear minded and farsighted individuals recognising the mutual benefits of improved transport to the port, (for the reasons already outlined) together with the development that would result. These benefits were promoted at a series of public meetings, finally resulting in the London and Southampton Railway Act of 1834 which cost the then colossal sum of £31,000 to promote.

Compared with railways then being projected in other parts of the country, the suggested route westwards as far as Basingstoke and then south-west to Southampton, would pose few problems to the engineer. Indeed, the only geological feature of note was the east-west contour of the chalk downs barring the path of the line between Basingstoke and Winchester. The engineer in charge was Francis Giles, later to be replaced by the redoubtable Joseph Locke. Giles had chosen a route through Basingstoke instead of what had been originally suggested south-west through Alton, so as to afford an easier connection with a proposed connection to Bath and Bristol. This was of course before the Great Western had secured their own act for a line from London to Bristol, the branch from Basingstoke being one of the rival suggestions.

Thus with Parliament having sanctioned the project, work was able to commence at several locations in late 1834. South of Winchester the route was engineered to take the course of the Itchen Valley with one David McIntosh responsible as contractor. North of the City and through as far as Basingstoke, Thomas Brassey was in charge, his name later being given to a residential road in the Fullflood area of Winchester and overlooking the line. Brassey was thus charged with the excavations and embankments through the chalk, some of these involving earthworks well in excess of 60 feet in variance compared with the original land contour.

Four tunnels were included in the section: Litchfield at 198 yards also being the summit of the long climb up from Eastleigh through Winchester; two at Micheldever (264 and 287 yards long respectively) and one at Wallers Ash of 497 yards. Those at Popham (Micheldever) were a compromise following a variation of the original plotted route in the area as the path would have taken the line much closer to

Micheldever village. This would have resulted in a single tunnel over 1 mile in length. The reasons for the deviation are complex in the extreme and were also to result in the replacement of Giles by Locke as engineer. Suffice it to say that certain of the inhabitants of the area did not wish to have a railway running so close to their land and so two

Worthy cutting c.1865 with Lovedon Lane bridge. This view illustrates the extremely steep chalk cutting, common to this line, which provides room for just single track despite the bridge being built to accommodate double track.

William Savage, courtesy Winchester City Museum

The Alton, Alresford and Winchester Railway (Mid-Hants) in the course of construction c.1863. This view is looking from Springvale towards Lovedon Lane bridge. Just beyond this point now exists the M3 motorway which directs the line.

William Savage, courtesy Winchester City Museum

separate villages developed each bearing similar names, Micheldever and Micheldever Station being some distance apart from one another.

But not all the wealthy land barons of the vicinity were against the new railway for one Sir Thomas Baring was so concerned as to the fate of the navvies who worked in what can only be described as primitive and extraordinarily dangerous conditions that he subscribed to the Hampshire County Hospital at Winchester where many of the unfortunates were taken. The actions of Sir Thomas were significant in that others were made aware of the conditions endured by the men and donations began to be accrued by the hospital; the railway company directors voting to donate £100. This was one of the first times an employer had provided what amounted to health care to his employees.

Nineteenth-Century Developments

With a new railway now running services into the existing Winchester station, the cramped environment of the stopping place became all the more of a nuisance to the operating department, especially so in view of the considerable build up of traffic that had occurred in the ensuing twenty years since the main line first opened. Those familiar with the geography of the station will be aware of its cramped situation, with cuttings either end and urban development encroaching onto the boundaries of railway land. There was thus little opportunity for expansion, but that is not to say the L & SWR did not try and whilst attempting to negotiate with a seemingly stubborn council (still, it appeared, in some ways averse to the railway age), they must have realised the hopelessness of the situation.

There was therefore little alternative but to attempt to improve the existing facilities without involving large scale expansion and hence over the following years the station was rebuilt to the form recognisable today. The pages of the various directors reports and committee minutes make fascinating reading, some of which are appended below:

14. 9.1865 New cattle pens to be provided.

11.10.1866 Complaint from an unknown source that passengers are having to cross over rails, and in so doing are exposed to danger.

31. 1.1867 Improved accommodation on the up platform, consisting of a small waiting room whilst the roof on this platform is to be extended. On the down side the platform is to be widened. To facilitate this work the existing cattle and horse docks to removed.

4. 5.1867 Letter received from a Mr. Hutchinson requesting a footbridge – not considered necessary at this time.

22.10.1868 Up platform to be lengthened by 100 feet.

17. 6.1869 A new brick signal box to be erected at the eastern end of the station.

15. 7.1869 Recommended that a new booking office be provided and equipped with 'ticket tubes' at a cost of £35–40. The old 'ticket cases' to be removed to supply other stations.

18.11.1869 Subway to be provided. Estimated cost £380.

Unfortunately, interesting though such references may be, they do not always provide full details of the circumstances leading up to the provision of new or revised facilities. Why for example was the decision made to build the subway? Why a subway and not a footbridge? Had there been a 'near miss' possibly involving Mr. Hutchinson? Likewise

were there any signalling facilities before 1869? Certainly with regard to physical items the answer can sometimes be obtained from a careful study of early maps, but as the period in question is before the first edition of Ordnance Survey, it is unlikely this source would be able to help.

The decade commencing 1870 saw further change, although as far as the City was concerned the main event was the attempt by the council to interest the L & SWR in siting their new Carriage and Wagon Works within the locality. Ironically, land was promised to accommodate this (one may wonder where this was to have been), yet other factions on the same council were still totally opposed to any request for further land for station expansion. It was clearly a left-hand/right-hand situation and hardly surprising that neighbouring Eastleigh later became the centre for carriage construction with the locomotive works also moving there a few years later. Alterations which did occur, however, included:

6. 1.1871 Removal of water crane from Winchester to be re-erected at Waterloo.

5.10.1871 New cattle dock approximately 50 feet in length.

21.12.1872 Sidings to be extended at a cost of £167.

26. 3.1874 Enlargement of goods shed, £45.

23. 8.1877 Enlargement of goods yard, £350.

The station at Winchester as it is today, really dates from 1886 onwards when the then not inconsiderable figure of £7,200 was spent on improvements concerning the conversion of the original offices on the down side into living accommodation for the Station Agent (sic), together with new buildings and a full complement of passenger facilities. As such the existing ramshackle collection of huts etc. were swept away on both sides, and the improvements completed by the adornment of a long wooden canopy covering the platform width as far as the trackwork. These facilities remained basically intact for more than 80 years until in the mid 1960s when the booking office and subway entrance, along with the former news stand, were rebuilt. (A further refurbishment occurred in 1987/8). Accordingly it may be of interest to relate the former changes in detail:

14. 3.1883 New works at Winchester in conjunction with the Hants and Berks agricultural show to be held in June 1883. The cattle loading dock in the eastern goods yard to be built at a maximum cost of £153.

9. 5.1883 New siding at a cost of £197.

23. 5.1883 Improved lighting to subway, £80.

6. 6.1883 Redecoration of station for visit by Prince and Princess of Wales to the Royal Agricultural Show.

13. 9.1883 Erection of cabmans shelter in Station Road. (sic).

28. 5.1884 Conversion of parcels office into refreshment room and erection of new parcels office, £542.

6. 8.1884 Lengthening of down platform by 100 feet at a cost of £112. At the same time a crossover worked from a ground frame to be moved.

6. 1.1886 General station improvements, £7,200.

.1886 New steps from the cab yard to Stockbridge Road.

1. 6.1887 Provision of a 50 Ton crane in the yard.

23. 1.1886 Extension of the goods shed. Estimated cost £707.

Despite only having their own muscle power and horses to construct the line, the section from Winchester as far as Southampton was completed in 1839 and opened amidst much ceremony on June 10th of that year, the same date as that from London as far west as Basingstoke. (Note: contemporary newspaper reports suggest that the opening may have been one week earlier on June 3rd). The following appeared in the Hampshire Chronicle:

"Winchester – Last Monday, the line of railway was opened to the public from Southampton to this city; and the novelty attracted hosts of spectators, not only inhabitants but those resident in the adjacent towns and villages. Soon after eight o'clock the first train arrived, the carriages filled with passengers, who on reaching the station, were received with acclamations from the assembled multitude. It was speedily found that the regular time of starting, previously announced, would not accommodate the number applying for places; and it was consequently resolved not only to place additional carriages on the road, but to run the trains from either end as fast as they could be got ready. It is calculated that upwards of 1200 persons passed to and fro in the course of the day. During the day Winchester exhibited a scene of bustle and animation, in consequence of the continued influx of visitors, anxious to witness the day. The country through which the line passes abounds in picturesque scenery and, after a delightful trip of some 20 minutes, the passengers alight at Southampton."

When the line opened there were stations at Winchester, Barton, (renamed Bishopstoke one year later and subsequently becoming Eastleigh) and Southampton. The terminus at Southampton was alongside Northam Bridge until the settlement of a dispute allowed the railway access to the intended Terminus station. North of Winchester work continued on the section to Basingstoke ,a general countrywide shortage of workers due to the massive railway building programme nationally not assisting the situation.

But at last all was finished, and the through line from London to Southampton opened amidst much ceremony on 11th May 1840; the newspapers of the day reported the event in several columns of text. Between Winchester and Basingstoke there was just one station, Andover Road, and as the name implies, a connection with a coach led to the latter location. The name persisted until 1854 when the direct route from Basingstoke westwards became available and the name Micheldever was substituted. Basingstoke nearly wasn't the chosen point of divergence, however, for there was strong support for a junction and line leading off westwards at Hook Pit (sic) whilst others favoured a connection near Micheldever. In the event, the area of Hook-pit, more correctly referred to as Springvale, was denied a railway junction although this was to come within a few decades.

Details of the first train services are somewhat vague, but what is recorded is one traveller's comment of being "whisked along at the astonishing speed of 30 mph", whilst the journey time between Winchester and London occupied between 1½ and 3 hours. When it is mentioned that such timings were accomplished without any form of signalling to regulate the passage of trains and that brakes were either primitive or non existent, the courage of the traveller must surely be wondered at! One amazing feature is that so few accidents occurred, although less than a week after opening there was an incident when the engine *Mercury* on the 10 a.m. from Nine Elms (London) to Southampton was derailed near Winchester killing both the driver and stoker (sic). Two years later, on 2nd April 1842, a fall in Wallers Ash Tunnel killed four workmen, the cause being put down to a vein of clay running through the chalk which had applied pressure to the roof lining until this had given way

WEEK DAY TRAINS.
TO FARNBOROUGH FOR ALDERSHOT, BASINGSTOKE, SOUTHAMPTON, WEYMOUTH, AND DORCHESTER.

DOWN.	1 2 3 class	Parl 1 2 3 class	1 2 class	* 1 2 class	Mail 1 2	Exp. 1 2	1 2 class	1 2 class	Exp. 1 2	1 2 class	* 1 2 class	Mail 1 2							
LEAVE					r				r	t	r								
WATERLOO BRIDGE	..	6 0	8 0	9 40	..	10 15	11 0	12 30	1 0	3 0	4 0	5 0	8 30	...	...	...	...	...	..
Vauxhall Bridge	..	6 8	..	9 46	..	..	..	12 36	..	..	..	..	..	...	...	...	...	...	...
Clapham Common	..	6 19	..	9 55	..	..	..	12 45	..	..	..	..	..	...	...	...	...	...	...
Wimbledon and Merton.........	..	6 29	..	10 8	..	..	..	12 53	..	..	..	..	..	...	...	...	...	...	...
Malden	..	6 38	..	..	..	..	..	..	..	..	..	..	..	...	...	...	...	...	...
Kingston	..	6 44	n	10 15	..	..	..	1 5	n	..	4 25	..	8 55	...	...	...	...	...	...
Esher and Claremont	..	6 53	..	10 23	..	..	..	1 12	..	..	4 32	..	9 3	...	...	...	...	...	...
Walton and Hersham	..	7 2	..	10 30	..	..	..	1 19	..	..	4 39	..	o	...	...	...	...	...	...
Weybridge	..	7 12	..	10 36	..	..	..	1 26	..	..	4 46	..	9 15	...	...	...	...	...	...
WOKING	...	7 30	s	10 50	..	11 3	..	1 38	1 47	..	4 58	..	9 28	!	...	...	...	...	...
Farnboro' for Aldershot ....dep.	..	8 0	8 55	11 20	..	..	..	2 5	..	..	5 18	5 56	9 48	...	...	...	...	...	...
Fleetpond	..	8 11	..	..	..	..	..	...	..	..	d	..	..	...	...	...	...	...	...
Winchfield	..	8 22	..	11 35	..	..	..	2 20	..	..	5 33	6 10	10 2	...	...	...	...	...	...
Basingstoke	..	8 46	9 20	11 55	..	12 15	..	2 40	4 15	5 50	6 30	10 18	..	...	...	...	...	...	...
Micheldever ....dep.	..	9 16	w	12 20	..	..	..	3 5	..	..	m	..	10 40	...	...	...	...	...	...
Winchester	..	9 36	9 54	12 37	12 50	..	..	3 25	4 50	..	7 6	..	10 56	...	...	...	...	...	...
Bishopstoke ....arr.	..	9 55	10 8	12 52	1 5	..	..	3 45	5 5	..	7 20	..	11 15	...	...	...	...	...	...
Bishopstoke ....dep.	...	9 57	10 10	12 54	1 7	..	..	3 47	5 7	..	7 22	..	11 17	...	...	...	...	...	...
SOUTHAMPTON DOCKS .... arr.	..	10 10	10 20	1 10	1 20	..	..	4 0	5 20	..	7 35	..	11 30	...	...	...	...	...	...
Ditto West End ......arr.					1 24				5 24		7 39								

	1 2 3 class	1 2 3 class.			h														
SOUTHAMPTON DOCKS ..dep.	6 0	10 30	..	..	..	..	..	..	..	..	..	12 6	..	...	...	...	...	...	...
Leave Bishopstoke	..	..	..	1 10	..	5 10	..	..	7 25	..	..	...	..	...	...	...	...	...	...
" Southampton, West End	6 6	10 36	..	1 24	..	5 24	..	..	7 39	..	..	...	..	...	...	...	...	...	...
Redbridge	6 13	10 43	..	1 30	..	5 30	..	..	7 44	..	12 19	..	..	...	...	...	...	...	...
Totton (for Eling)	6 15	10 45	..	1 32	..	5 32	..	..	7 46	..	12 21	..	..	...	...	...	...	...	...
Lyndhurst Road	6 24	10 54	..	1 39	..	5 39	..	..	7 52	..	..	...	..	...	...	...	...	...	...
Beaulieu Road	6 32	11 2	..	..	..	5 44	..	..	..	..	..	...	..	...	...	...	...	...	...
Brockenhurst (Lymington Junction)	6 45	11 15	..	1 57	..	5 53	..	..	8 6	..	12 48	..	..	...	...	...	...	...	...
Lym. Br. Lymington { ......arr. / ....dep.	7 5 / 6 25	11 30 / 11 0	..	2 10 / 1 40	..	6 10 / 5 40	..	..	8 25 / 7 45	..	..	...	..	...	...	...	...	...	...
Christchurch Road	7 0	11 29	..	2 9	..	6 8	..	..	8 17	..	..	...	..	...	...	...	...	...	...
Ringwood	7 16	11 45	..	2 21	..	6 20	..	..	8 30	..	1 19	..	..	...	...	...	...	...	...
Wimborne	7 41	12 10	..	2 40	..	6 39	..	..	8 48	..	1 45	..	..	...	...	...	...	...	...
POOLE Junction	7 57	12 26	..	2 54	..	6 51	..	..	9 2	..	2 5	..	..	...	...	...	...	...	...
Poole Br. POOLE { ......arr. / ....dep.	8 15 / 7 45	12 40 / 12 15	..	3 12 / 2 42	..	7 5 / 6 40	..	..	9 15 / 8 50	..	2 19	..	..	...	...	...	...	...	...
Wareham	8 12	12 41	..	3 8	..	7 2	..	..	9 13	..	2 19	..	..	...	...	...	...	...	...
Wool	8 30	1 1	..	h	..	1	..	..	...	..	..	...	..	...	...	...	...	...	...
Moreton	8 50	1 14	..	h	..	..	..	..	9 38	..	..	...	..	...	...	...	...	...	...
DORCHESTER ....arr.	9 5	1 29	..	3 42	..	7 37	..	..	9 50	3 5	..	...	..	...	...	...	...	...	...
WEYMOUTH ....arr.	9 30	1 50	..	4 0	..	8 0	..	..	10 5	g	..	...	..	...	...	...	...	...	...

* OMNIBUSES leave the Spread Eagle, Gracechurch Street, City, half an hour before the departure of these Trains from Waterloo Bridge Station.
The Time of the Mail Trains are fixed by the Post Master General.
r This mark indicates the Train does not proceed beyond the Station on the same Line.
d This Train will stop at Fleetpond to put down any London Passenger who has previously communicated his destination to the Superintendent at Waterloo Bridge Station.
The passengers by this Train from Wareham and Moreton must change Carriages at Wareham.
h This Train for Wool and Moreton will run between Dorchester and Weymouth on Sunday and Thursdays only.
m This Train stops on Mondays at Micheldever to set down London Passenger.
‡ This Train will stop at Kingston by Signal to set down London Passengers.
d This Train will stop at Walton for London Passengers who give notice to 6½ Guard before leaving Waterloo.
‖ This Train will stop at Woking to set down Passengers who are conveyed by the 11 a.m. or 3 p.m. and 5 p.m. Down Trains.
t This Train will stop from Farnborough and Southampton only.
This is a Third Class Train from Basingstoke and at Woking.
w This Train will stop on Saturdays at Micheldever to set down Passengers from London.

with fatal consequences. The line was re-opened to trains only two days later and whilst a later small fall was recorded at the same spot no further trouble was experienced.

With the population provided with an accessible and affordable means of rapid transport, for both passengers and goods, the days of the canals and stage coaches were numbered. The latter succumbed very early on whilst the canal owners struggled manfully until forced to concede against what were insurmountable odds. So it was in 1869 that the Itchen Navigation finally ceased operation as a navigable waterway, whilst elsewhere in the county railways were being built in ever-increasing numbers, even, ironically, as in the case of the Andover and Redbridge, on the course of a projected but never completed waterway.

The Alton Line

Locally the nominally independent, Alton, Alresford and Winchester Railway had, in 1861, obtained their Act for powers to build a 17-mile line from Alton to a junction with the main line two miles north of Winchester. The actual point of divergence was known as Winchester Junction and is now within the parish of Springvale/Kings Worthy. The branch was opened on 2nd October 1865, its name having in the meantime been changed to the Mid-Hants Railway Company. The London & South Western Railway (formerly the London & Southampton) worked the new line from the start and finally absorbed it outright in 1876.

In common with the main line, the new route possessed the characteristic deep cuttings and high embankments of a route traversing the chalk ridge, and whilst only a single line of track was laid, sufficient land had been purchased to allow for doubling should it become necessary. Even so,

with the almost unbroken procession of earthworks between Winchester Junction and the first station at Itchen Abbas, such work would have been highly expensive.

Having briefly spoken of the rebuilding work undertaken at Winchester, it is now time to turn to the activities taking place elsewhere, and in particular a plan of 1873 for a railway running almost directly north–south from the Great Western at Didcot to a junction with the South Western just north of Micheldever. This was in fact the first scheme later to result in the Didcot, Newbury and Southampton line. But as previously mentioned, the area around Micheldever was noted for its deep cuttings and because the company wished to reach Southampton, the aims were soon changed to that of an independent route south from Newbury through Winchester to the port.

Accordingly, on 1st May 1885, the independent DN & S opened their route from Newbury as far as Winchester where, for the time being at least, a terminus was to exist (see chapter 2). The two Winchester stations were approximately one mile apart on an east–west basis. With the avowed intention of the newcomer to reach Southampton independently of the L & SWR, it is easy to understand the opposition begun by the latter concern when facing a possible end to their erstwhile monopoly of traffic. Thus there begins one of the most amazing stories of railway rivalry, counter espionage and deceit seen in Hampshire, more of which is said in the following chapter. Suffice it to say that in 1882, when Shawford station had been opened some three miles south of Winchester, the threat of the rival had been recognised even then with their proposed station at nearby Twyford. Hence the name displayed made no reference to Twyford at all, a situation persisting to this day despite the timetables showing Shawford for Twyford.

A striking view of Station Hill and old Winchester c.1909. The horse drawn carriage is one of two regularly plying between the railway and one or two hostels to generate trade. This particular vehicle is believed to be destined for the Royal Hotel in St Peter Street. The wooden building to the right was originally a mission hall, later to become a taxi office and after that to be used by one of the coal merchants.

D.C. Dine collection

H.R.H. King George V and Queen Mary at Winchester on the occasion of their visit on 15th July 1912. Their Royal Highnesses were to attend a service of thanksgiving in the Cathedral for the restoration work carried out on the building. *Ian Best Collection*

There had been a clamour for a station at Shawford for at least 20 years before one was to open and why such a delay persisted before the directors finally agreed to accede to the requests remains unclear. In the event Shawford station was built at a cost of £3,580 with the work, it is recorded, being carried out by the company's own men.

With the opening of Otterbourne siding, a little way south of Shawford, in 1885, and the connection between the DN & S and L & SWR at Shawford Junction in 1891, the railway picture of the area is almost complete. The following years witnessed a succession of moves towards consolidation rather than expansion. But changes were on the way with a society that had begun the course along the way towards motor vehicle dependence.

Twentieth Century Development

Edwardian Winchester was a pleasing, well-to-do community, boasting opportunities for those from all social echelons. At the one end of the spectrum were the professionals and scholars involved in the running and administration of the famous Cathedral and College, whilst further down the social scale the opportunist found plenty to exercise his business acumen in what was still a tranquil yet favourable environment. In consequence, the train service developed also, a glance at the timetable showing how trains to London for example compared with that of years gone by.

But despite the fortunes of the railway companies reaching their peak in the years prior to World War 1, the L & SWR seemed disinclined to respond to requests for new stations in the area at Otterbourne and Kings Worthy on the Mid Hants line between Itchen Abbas and Winchester Junction. With regard to the former, this would only have had minimal patronage, for although goods traffic, and in particular coal to the Southampton Corporation Waterworks was on the increase, it is very unlikely if sufficient patronage would have been forthcoming at a passenger station. But at Kings Worthy it was a different matter, for the L & SWR here lost an opportunity to tap the potentially rich pickings from the Springvale end of the area. The requests for a stopping place on the Alton line at this point were heard right up to the time this line closed in the 1970s.

The First World War

Such a tranquil and peaceful way of life changed beyond recognition in August 1914 when war broke out on a scale never before seen. So far as the South Western was concerned there were immediate and continuing demands upon their facilities, the cramped layout at Winchester again being called into question. This was especially so with the establishment of several large army camps within the area: Flowerdown, Hazeley Down, Hursley Park and Morn Hill to name but four. Later of course the last named was to receive direct rail access off of the DN & S line but there was an urgent demand for increased facilities at the main line station as well.

Accordingly, in the up side yard, additional goods shed and office accommodation were provided together with a second-hand 10 ton crane and increased facilities for loading horses and vehicles. The cost of all this was recorded at some £1,400. Such improvements though did little to relieve the problem of entraining troops and a compromise solution reached, as late as 1918, was the construction of a platform alongside the 'Baltic Siding' north of the Andover Road bridge. This was costed at £2,797 with much of the work being carried out by servicemen from the Morn Hill camp. The work also included track and signal alterations so as to permit troop trains to enter and leave the platform from either direction. But to do so a move across the running lines was involved and when the facilities were subsequently inspected by the Board of Trade the matter came in for some criticism. Possibly for this reason the facilities remained in use for only a short period, although the name of the 'Baltic Sidings' remains to this day. Hardly of relevance to the war effort was the South Western's approval to a request for a bath to be installed in the Station House. This was carried out in 1917 at a cost of £48!

The Return of Peace

With a return to peace, social needs and in particular a lack of available council housing within the City resulted in a large scale building programme in the area to be known as Lower Stanmore. To bring in materials for this, a siding was installed at a cost of £4,700 to the council, trailing off the up line near to Ranelagh Road bridge. This then dropped down sharply to the land level after which two sidings led off to various unloading points. All traces of the site have now been obliterated.

Hardly the fault of the railway companies, but the return to peace found the lines and stock in a run down and dejected condition, the directors being unable to restore pre-war standards due to shortages of both manpower and finance. The resulting discontentment affected both passengers and staff, culminating in a strike of railway workers during the later part of 1919. Volunteers were sought to maintain a service of sorts but in so doing there were bound to be incidents, one occurring at Winchester on 4th October

The area has been relatively free from accidents, apart of course from the usual indiscretions and minor calamities inseparable from a working railway. Of these, potentially the most serious was in December 1923 when a luggage trolley fell of the platform edge at Winchester into the path of a train which at the time was less than 150 yards away and with no chance of stopping in that short distance. Miraculously the only damage was to the timber of the trolley, unlike at Wellingborough on the Midland Railway in 1898, where under similar circumstances, seven persons were killed. But there has also been tragedy locally too with several recorded incidents of persons walking or straying on the line and being struck by trains.

of that year when the 4.55 p.m. Southampton West to Winchester train was derailed whilst running round at Winchester station. A non-striking driver and volunteer naval foreman were on the footplate, the latter misreading the indication given by a ground signal, fortunately without serious consequences.

WINCHESTER (L&SWR) – WORLD WAR I SCENES

A touching gesture at Winchester South Western during World War I. *Imperial War Museum*

Despite the existence of the troop platform, trains for embarkation were still dealt with at the main Winchester station as seen here on the down side. *Imperial War Museum*

THE WORLD WAR I TROOP PLATFORM

▲The troop platform north of Andover Road bridge under construction in 1918. Labour for this was mainly in the form of American servicemen billeted at Morn Hill and survivors from the sinking of their troopship in the North Atlantic. At the north end a small signal box controlled the exit onto the main line and whilst no other details of this have emerged the box would most likely to have been of timber construction and giving the appearance of a temporary structure. *Imperial War Museum*

►Work on the platform continuing, this time viewed towards Andover Road overbridge.*Imperial War Museum*

CHAPTER 2

THE DIDCOT NEWBURY AND SOUTHAMPTON

Alternative Proposals

The first proposals for a north–south railway connection through Hampshire are traceable back to the period of the railway mania, when the grandiose-sounding Manchester and Southampton scheme proposed a line linking the two places. The Manchester and Southampton idea was really only a way to link existing railways between Cheltenham and Southampton, and so failed due to being unable to live up to the desires of those it had been intended to serve.

But in so doing, the seed for such a route had been sown and the early 1870s saw a revival of interest in improving the links between the industrial Midlands and the South. The fundamental problem of a change in gauge, brought about by the construction of the Great Western Railway to Brunel's broad gauge, had been overcome by laying mixed gauge from Oxford to Basingstoke but the route was somewhat circuitous with the line going via Reading. A scheme for a direct line was therefore seen as desirable and in 1873 a Bill was sought for the Didcot, Newbury and Southampton Junction Railway.

Disagreements with the South Western over a connection at Micheldever and consequent running powers to Southampton caused the DN & SJR directors to seek an independent approach to the port, the proposed new route running through Whitchurch, Sutton Scotney, Winchester, Twyford, Allbrook, Chandler's Ford and Chilworth to a terminus near the Royal Pier at Southampton.

The promoters of the DN & S (the word 'Junction' was dropped from the title eventually) always considered their line to be first and foremost an important through route, having the advantage of a saving of some six miles compared with the Reading and Basingstoke route. The company were soon to realise their naivity in the matter of railway politics as the interests of the large and established GWR and L & SWR although at variance with each other, found common ground in stifling the establishment of the small but ambitious DN & S. An agreement was made, however, with the GWR for working the new line, this covering the working of all trains as well as the provision of staff at the stations in return for a percentage of gross receipts. Such an agreement was commonplace amongst small railway companies as it allowed them to concentrate their efforts on land and construction without having the additional burden of the cost of locomotives and rolling stock. But there was also the risk that the working company could take advantage of the situation, as referred to by the DN & S traffic manager, Mr. W.H.H.M. Gipps.:

'It should be borne in mind that the object of a big railway company in working a line is usually to afford the barest possible service, and do nothing to augment its value in view of its probably passing at some future date into their own hands.'

How right Gipps was, but fate would decree that he was not to live to see his prophecy come true.

The Line Opens

With the first section of the line between Didcot and Newbury opened for traffic and no agreement with the L & SWR over access to Southampton, the drive was on for an independent approach to the port. However because it was decided to reach Winchester at all costs all work at Southampton ceased from November 1883 onwards and it was never to resume.

So it was in the spring of 1885 that the little line reached Winchester, the final approach being made through a 441-yard tunnel under St. Giles Hill to a station tucked away to one side of Chesil Street, the only place where land could be purchased at a price the company could afford.

As was customary, grandiose celebrations were held to mark the occasion of the opening, contemporary press reports providing a valuable insight into not only these events but also the original facilities as provided:

"THE OPENING CEREMONY AT WINCHESTER"

"The special was due at Winchester at 2.45, but did not arrive till half an hour later, the start from Newbury having been delayed. An eager crowd had collected to welcome the travellers, streaming from behind the lofty paling which ran along down the edge of the cutting, filling the parapet above the tunnel, lining the palings along the steep where stands the station master's red house, and filling the approach to the station. Two enterprising photographers, it was said, from Portsmouth had perched themselves on the station wall at the base of St. Giles's Hill, instruments in hand, ready to take instantaneous pictures of the returning train and its occupants. The weather which had improved since the morning, was now positively fine, and the sun shone out from the clear blue in unclouded splendour. Just as the Guildhall clock struck three the train emerged from the tunnel, and was received with great cheering which was again and again taken up. It took some time for the passengers to disembark. Then the Winchester Corporation kept the ground to the marquee, into which mayors, aldermen, and other distinguished persons were pouring till its capacity was tested to the very utmost extent. Along those present were Lord Baring, M.P. and Lady Emma Baring, Sir Loyd Lindsay, and Lady Loyd Lindsay, Mr. Baxton, M.P. and Mrs. Baxton, Mr. J. Fowler, the Mayor of Winchester, Aldermen Budden and Godwin &c. The Mayor congratulated them on behalf of the citizens of Winchester that this undertaking had been so far completed to this ancient city, and he trusted they would have the pleasure before long to see it brought down to the town of Southampton. On behalf of the citizens and Corporation of Winchester he begged to thank them for their presence there that day, and trusted that the line would add to the prosperity of Winchester and the district. (Cheers). Lord Baring then escorted Lady Loyd Lindsay to the front of the marquee, and her ladyship formally declared the line open and wished it, amid loud cheers, God-speed. Lord Baring thanked her ladyship on behalf of the chairman and directors of the company.

The lower part of the city to which the events of the day were chiefly confined had made preparations for the occasion by turning out all the flags and banners it could apparently muster, which spanned the High-street in various places, floated on the top of the Guildhall, and from poles in the Broadway, and depended from numerous windows. The only attempt at house decoration was made by Bishop Brothers, the front of whose premises was set off with great taste with trophies of flags and wreaths of evergreens, as became an establishment the head of which is the Mayor of Southampton.

As you approached the railway station the decorations became more and more profuse. The pavement was lined at intervals with trophies of flags, and at each side of the city bridge were erected triumphal arches, dressed with evergreens and gay drapery, that on the city side bearing in white letters on crimson the motto, "Success to the new railway, and may it soon reach Southampton." In Bridge-street the Bridge Inn was set off with flags and evergreens, and almost from every window hung a symbol of some kind. Water-lane modestly veiled its attractions by a string of flags suspended at the entrance; and similar decorations spanned the entrance to Cheesehill-street and the path to St. Giles's Hill. The residence of the city surveyor, Mr. Gamon, in Cheesehill-street, fronting the entrance to the station, was conspicuous for its exceedingly tasteful decorations of white flowers and evergreens in which every window was framed. The station entrance exhibited gay bunting everywhere, and the station itself was very prettily decked with flowers, and evergreens wreathed the pillars and arched the openings. At the lower end near the tunnel was erected a handsome marquee of white and red cloth for the reception of Lady Loyd Lindsay on the occasion of her formally declaring the line open."

"GOING TO NEWBURY"

"At ten o'clock the members of Corporations of the city and Southampton began to assemble at the Guildhall in accordance with the printed programme. The Mayor of Winchester (W.T. Warren, Esq.). welcomed the visitors as they arrived in mackintoshes under wet umbrellas to enjoy the festive holiday. The scene from the Guildhall steps was not at this moment a cheerful one, and required a Mark Tapley to regard it with kindly feelings. The rain kept steadily descending, and the pavements were covered by a melancholy crowd of dripping sightseers. At half-past ten the Mayors and Corporations of Southampton and Winchester, all in state, with their town clerks, mace bearers, and other officials, formed in procession, two deep, and headed by the band of the Hampshire Regiment marched to the station, under a penthouse of umbrellas, followed by a numerous crowd undeterred by the downpour and the sloppy streets. Between five and six hundred invitations had been issued by the directors to the shareholders and others to join them in the opening trip to Newbury, and for that number a special train, consisting of a saloon carriage, four first class, twelve second and third class carriages, and three break-vans (sic) were provided by the Great Western Railway. The

arrangement of carriages was somewhat criticised, but the truth is the second were not greatly inferior to the first, nor the second much superior to the third. On the arrival of the procession the train speedily filled and proceeded on its journey under the charge of Inspector Upchurch of Reading."

Public services to Newbury commenced on 4th May 1885, with four trains each way weekdays, provided of course by the GWR. Attention now turned to recommencing work on the Southampton extension and in this connection the Directors report to the shareholders at the June 1885 meeting said that a further £100,000 was required. Little difficulty was anticipated gathering this sum with the work as planned to be completed within two years.

However, this optimism was not to be matched by investors despite the councils of Winchester and Southampton subscribing £15,000 and £70,000 respectively. These sums were quickly eaten up in going towards operating costs, the line as it stood being unable to attract sufficient traffic to even cover costs.

The Company was thus in a cleft stick; it could not attract sufficient funds to reach Southampton and yet unless it somehow managed to do so the growth in traffic would never materialise with the line terminating in a quiet backwater. Nor would either of the two larger concerns assist for fear of antagonism in other areas. But the South Western at least was shrewd enough to recognise that until a satisfactory conclusion was reached there was always the risk of the situation changing, especially if relations with the GWR took an unexpected turn for the worse. They then came up with an olive branch in the form of finance to construct a connection with their own line just north of Shawford station at a point to become known as Shawford Junction. In return, the DN & S had to agree to abandon any attempt to an independent approach to Southampton. Faced with such a proposition it is understandable that there was conflict amongst the shareholders but the result was inevitable and the 2 miles 6 chains railway linking the DN & S at Bar End with the South Western at Shawford Junction was opened without ceremony on 1st January 1891. Through services to the coast could begin at last.

From St. Catherines Hill, and long before the Winchester by-pass, rail and waterway run parallel with 'Tunbridge' visible in the background.

Graham Hawkins collection

Kings Worthy station as opened to traffic and looking north towards Sutton Scotney (Worthy Down was not at this time built). The Winchester–Basingstoke road runs under the railway at right angles at the far end of the platform, the signalman having a good view of traffic on this road as well as approaching trains. There is a suggestion that there may have been a crossing loop at this point before the station was opened in 1909, but no evidence to support this theory has yet come to light. *Lens of Sutton*

The Didcot, Newbury and Southampton line timetable with effect from Thursday 1st October 1891 and the opening of the connection from Winchester to Shawford Junction. The mention of Shawford Junction on what was a public notice is of interest. Was there perhaps a ticket platform at the junction? – perhaps unlikely. But certainly the other junctions viz Didcot East, Newbury East and Enborne are not shown.

Didcot, Newbury, Winchester, and Southampton.

DOWN TRAINS.

		A.M.	A.M. 1,2,p	P.M.	P.M. 1,2,p
DIDCOT	Dep.	7.45		1.10	6.20
Upton	,,	7.54		1.19	6.29
Compton	,,	8.7		1.32	6.42
Hampstead Norris	,,	8.12		1.37	6.47
Hermitage	,,	8.20		1.45	6.55
NEWBURY	Arr.	8.30		1.55	7.5
NEWBURY	Dep.	8.58	11.25	2.15	7.15
Woodhay	,,	9.7	11.34	2.24	7.24
Highclere	,,	9.16	11.43	2.33	7.33
Burghclere	,,	9.22	11.49	2.39	7.39
Litchfield	,,	9.29	11.56	2.48	7.46
Whitchurch	,,	9.37	12.4	2.56	7.54
Sutton Scotney	,,	9.48	12.15	3.7	8.5
WINCHESTER	Arr.	10.1	12.28	3.20	8.18
WINCHESTER	Dep.	10.20	12.38	3.28	8.28
Shawford Junction	,,	10.25	12.43	3.33	8.33
Shawford	,,	10.30	12.47	3.37	8.37
Eastleigh	,,	10.38	12.55	3.44	8.45
Swathling	,,	10.43	1.0	3.49	8.50
St. Denys	,,	10.47	1.4	3.53	8.54
Northam	,,	10.52	1.9	3.58	8.59
SOUTHAMPTON	Arr.	10.55	1.12	4.1	9.2

SUN. A Mixed Train leaves Whitchurch at 6.45 and Sutton Scotney at 7.10 a.m. for Winchester.

On Tuesdays, Wednesdays, Thursdays, Fridays, and Saturdays a Mixed Train leaves Whitchurch at 6.45 a.m., and Sutton Scotney at 7.10 a.m. for Winchester.

Didcot, Newbury, Winchester, and Southampton.

UP TRAINS. — WEEK DAYS ONLY.

		A.M. 1,2,p	A.M.	P.M.	P.M. 1,2,p
SOUTHAMPTON	Dep.	6.55	9.30	1.20	4.35
Northam	,,	6.59	9.34	1.24	4.38
St. Denys	,,	7.4	9.38	1.28	4.42
Swathling	,,	7.9	9.43	1.33	4.47
Eastleigh	,,	7.16	9.50	1.40	4.53
Shawford	,,	7.25	9.59	1.49	5.2
Shawford Junction	,,	7.28	10.2	1.52	5.5
WINCHESTER	Arr.	7.33	10.7	1.57	5.10
WINCHESTER	Dep.	7.40	10.20	2.10	5.20
Sutton Scotney	,,	7.56	10.36	2.26	5.36
Whitchurch	,,	8.8	10.48	2.38	5.48
Litchfield	,,	8.18	10.58	2.48	5.58
Burghclere	,,	8.25	11.5	2.55	6.5
Highclere	,,	8.30	11.10	3.0	6.10
Woodhay	,,	8.36	11.16	3.6	6.16
NEWBURY	Arr.	8.45	11.25	3.15	6.25
NEWBURY	Dep.	9.20	11.28	3.35	6.45
Hermitage	,,	9.30	11.38	3.45	6.55
Hampstead Norris	,,	9.38	11.46	3.53	7.3
Compton	,,	9.45	11.53	4.0	7.10
Upton	,,	9.57	12.5	4.12	7.22
DIDCOT	Arr.	10.5	12.13	4.20	7.30

For the convenience of Passengers a carriage will be attached to the Goods Train leaving Winchester at 7.5 p.m., and Newbury at 10.0 p.m., for Didcot. This Train will call at all Stations.

Improvements

The next few years saw some improvement in the Company's fortunes, but the dreams of the promoters of their line becoming a trunk route were somewhat muted by the attitude of the larger companies who saw it as an encumbrance and purely a local line serving the sparsely populated areas of North Hampshire and the Berkshire downs. Despite this, the DN & S remained resolute and were frequently at odds with the GWR over many matters, not the least of which was the basic train service provided, which became a constant source of frustration to the company.

The year 1905 saw the first of additional facilities on the railway with new works for the Winchester Water and Gas Company opened at Winnall on 2nd September; this concern previously having occupied cramped facilities in Staple Gardens. In connection with this, a new private siding was laid for the firm's use and regular trips of coal wagons from the goods yard at Bar End to the siding became a common feature. In consequence tar and coke were also dealt with.

As far back as 1893, following requests from local residents, the DN & S agreed to provide a station at Kings Worthy. This would have been a very modest affair, but the plans were changed to allow for a more substantial structure which was finally opened to passengers on 1st February 1909. The station proved to be a well justified investment to the little company, for over the years a good deal of traffic was dealt with including farm produce, race horses from several local studs, and heavy machinery from the Kings Worthy foundry.

Some eight years later a further stopping place was opened at Worthy Down near the site of the former Winchester racecourse. Here the Royal Flying Corps had established a camp, the basic station facilities somehow matching the flimsy aircraft seen bouncing around like paper darts tossed in the wind. The crude facilities were opened on 1st April 1918, a date that may have made people think the DN & S was purporting a practical joke to suggest this was indeed a station. A minor improvement was carried out in the early 1920s when the old horse box body serving as a booking office was replaced by a corrugated iron hut with the additional benefit of a canopy shelter. However, it was not to be until the later improvements of 1942/3 before proper waiting facilities became available.

The Wartime Link to Winnall Downs

The outbreak of war in 1914 at long last justified the claims of the promoters that the DN & S could become an important through route and together with its neighbour the Midland and South Western Junction from Cheltenham to Andover it assumed a strategic importance in the transportation of the men and accoutrements of war to the south coast ports. A considerable amount of military traffic was thus dealt with including ambulance trains, often destined for the temporary military hospitals established at Burghclere and Highclere. Some of this rather sad traffic was also handled at Winchester GW where wounded soldiers were laid out the length of the up platform prior to being stretchered into vehicles taking them to the Royal Hampshire County Hospital.

The establishment later in the War of the large military camps stretching across from Morn Hill and Winnall Down to Avington Park is nowadays fairly well known. More obscure is the rail link that was laid from the DN & S north of the Winchester Tunnel to serve the camps, the junction brought into use on 20th October 1918. First mention of rail access to the camps comes in a letter of 29th April 1918 from the General Manager of the GWR to a Mr. Beresford-Turner, in that consideration was being given to using the DN & S for the passage of heavy traffic to and from the camps. He went on to say that the War Office had concluded that the original scheme for access was too elaborate and costly, but tantalisingly no records to detail this first proposal appear to have survived. The new link, as originally built, was some three miles in length and worked on the basis of a long siding.

About 270,000 servicemen were accommodated at the three main camps, the men being of varying nationalities but primarily Americans. A large contingent of these was responsible for the construction of the railway itself. The line was used for the delivery of military supplies, provender for the numerous horses, and coal and flour for the bakery at Winnall Down Camp, which itself supplied the other establishments. Here especially, employment was provided for many local civilians, both women and youths engaged on canteen and general domestic duties.

As demobilisation of men returning from the front drew to a close, the camps were drastically reduced in size and the usefulness of the railway began to decline. By late 1920 it was out of use although the rails were not lifted until three years later. Although its history was brief it was not without incident as on one occasion a local man was killed in an accident involving some bricklaying work in connection with the railway during 1919. The steep climb from the junction with the DN & S across the Winnall Downs and around the back of Victoria Hospital was the cause of another incident when sixteen wagons ran back after the brakes had failed, finishing up in a tangled mess at the catch point by the junction, fortunately on this occasion without human injury. With the camps out of use, the buildings, mainly of corrugated construction, were sold off. Many of these sales were conducted by the Auctioneers James Harris and proved to be a popular venture for the local citizens, for several purchased buildings which were later transported to the Springvale area for re-erection in a different form as bungalows, others finding a similar role at Monkwood near Ropley.

Construction work on the camp line from the DN & S to Morn Hill, shown here curving around Winnall Down in 1918. The labour again provided by American servicemen.
Imperial War Museum

CHAPTER 3

THE RAILWAYS OF WINCHESTER AFTER THE GROUPING

The Southern Lines

The Railways Act of 1921, intended by Government to make the railways more efficient by grouping them into larger concerns, had amalgamated the L & SWR into the Southern Railway, the change taking effect from 1st January 1923. In the same year the new owners undertook a feasibility study regarding a new halt at St. Cross, with an alternative to close the level crossing and divert the pathway along to nearby Stanmore Lane. A plan of the former is shown on page 00. Both schemes came to nothing.

The following decade saw the SR effecting few changes locally and instead concentrating on developments else-where, like the expansion of Southampton Docks. But the period was also to witness a slow slide towards the depression of the 1930s which although having serious consequences elsewhere, had little effect on this, one of England's southernmost shires.

Although able to weather the economic storm better than most, the SR was in competition with the road hauliers and whilst the motor operators were unable to compete with regard to rates and speeds over any distance, the directors were acutely aware that their monopoly was at last being threatened. Added to this, rising operating costs and falling receipts meant it was inevitable that economies would have to be made. The 1930s then saw the first of a series of closures affecting minor lines. In Hampshire alone these included the Basingstoke–Alton, Lee-on-the-Solent–Hurstbourne–Fullerton and Ringwood–Christchurch lines all closing to passengers. In most cases a railway closing was something of a novelty and was thus well reported in the local press.

But it was not a question of cut backs on the main line, for the main line services, and in particular at holiday times, were so well patronised that the Southern were forced to increase line capacity, although this made the various bottlenecks even more acute. Consequently, in 1931, quadrupling of the main line was completed from Shawford to Eastleigh, although the six years it had taken to complete the work is perhaps a reflection of the prevailing economic climate. Around the same time serious consideration was given to a means of by-passing the Southern station at Winchester with the building of a link to allow southbound trains direct access to the Great Western line at Kings Worthy and so through Winchester Chesil, to link back into the main line at Shawford Junction. For reasons not recorded the idea was not proceeded with, although it may well have had something to do with the advantages to be gained being outweighed by the disadvantages of the slow speed caused by the single track sections on the GWR line.

Ironically, the next suggestion was to abandon the DN & S, through Kings Worthy and Winchester and by means of a different connecting spur, divert all trains onto the SR main line. The idea then was to use the trackbed of the abandoned railway for the route of the projected Winchester by-pass. This scheme, however, was vetoed by the War Office after apparently having found favour with the railway companies. Again though it raises the question of how the main line would have coped.

With the advent of the second world war, increased demands were again made upon the local railway system. Winchester 'Southern' had a loading platform built in the down yard for the movement of tanks and other heavy vehicles onto rail transport. On the passenger platforms too

For many years there were through Waterloo–Southampton trains via Alton, whilst after the introduction of the diesel service it was still a pleasurable way to reach 'town' provided one was not in too much of a hurry. Here one of the earlier steam services heads south from Winchester Junction with a Southampton via Alton service; in charge is U class 2–6–0 No. A 612. *Author's collection*

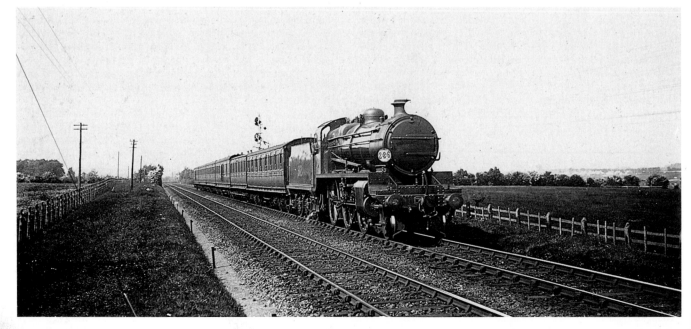

To facilitate the unloading of tanks and other large vehicles at Winchester Southern during World War II, a loading bank was quickly built to the rear of the signal box in the down yard. This view shows it to advantage. *British Railways*

A northbound train in the charge of an ex LSWR T14 class 4–6–0 No. 443 passing the down starting signal around 1936. In later years, following the removal of the connecting sidings at this point, the cutting sides have shallowed and now reach the up running line. *G.R.L. Coles*

there were changes, with a public address system being installed for the first time. Other than this the only other item of major significance was the extension of the down relief line from Shawford back towards Shawford Junction at a cost of some £50,129. Both up and down relief lines at Shawford were classified as 'permissive goods lines' meaning they could be used for storage of freight trains nose to tail if necessary. Meanwhile at Winchester Junction a link between the two companies' lines was at last completed, ironically in a different place from all the previous proposals. This allowed northbound GWR trains direct access from the SR main line but it did not take an engineer to realise that it was also an insurance should enemy action render the tunnel or the vulnerable viaduct impassable. All the wartime works were chargeable to the Government.

Fortunately the years of conflict resulted in little damage to the area, the City spared the terrible torments of its near neighbours Portsmouth and Southampton. But the return to peace was recognisable by a legacy of arrears in maintenance and rolling stock renewal. Add to this the demands made by a travelling public now freed from the constraints of war, yet still hampered by petrol rationing, and one may perhaps realise the difficulties faced by the railway companies.

The result was the socialist government decision to nationalise the complete network, the Southern Railway becoming the Southern Region of British Railways as from January 1st 1948. Great things were promised, above all a railway system for the future. How and what actually happened in the form of change is the subject of the final chapter.

The GWR Line

The independence of the DN & S came to and end with the grouping of railways in 1923, it now forming part of the GWR proper. But as this company already provided the trains and staff there was little actual difference to the casual traveller. Indeed, the occasion is best recollected by an irate shareholder from Bournemouth who wrote complaining that out of his original investment he had not received a penny dividend, a similar fate having affected many others.

The decision to relieve Winchester of the ever increasing burden of road traffic in the early 1930s raised the subject of the future of the line south of Worthy Down. Land around the City was at a premium and few options were open to the authorities as to the provision of a suitable by-pass. As mentioned in the preceding chapter, the suggestion was mooted to abandon the line south of Worthy Down and divert all trains onto the Southern line by the construction of a new spur. In the event a compromise was reached and between Bar End and Hockley the railway was moved sideways by some 55 feet where it passed around St. Catherines Hill, the new road being sandwiched between the foot of the hill and the railway. The necessary excavations made deep inroads into the hillside and the legacy of this action is still present half a century later and accounts for the extreme narrowness of the dual carriageway at this point.

The outbreak of the war in 1939 once again reaffirmed the importance of the line as a vital link in the transport chain. A steady build up of trains used the route, most of these in a southerly direction. Fundamental changes in the outward appearance of the railway were on the way, when in 1942 the military authorities took the decision to undertake major improvements along the whole route from Didcot to Winchester and so significantly increase the route capacity. This work, commenced in August 1942, took the form of doubling the existing single line from Didcot to

Newbury and south as far as Woodhay and extending crossing loops at all the stations beyond that point. At Winchester, the tunnel had fortunately been constructed with provision for double track and so for the first time since the railway was opened this was doubled throughout. The connections to the former camps at Morn Hill were not, however, restored.

At Worthy Down the station was completely reconstructed, with a new island platform, waiting shelter and office. A new spur was also put in from the Southern main line at Winchester Junction and allowed northbound trains to leave the main line and rejoin the DN & S route just south of Worthy Down. Total cost of the new works between Didcot and Winchester amounted to some £564,720, a not inconsiderable figure and perhaps reflecting the importance placed on the line by the government. It seemed, even if somewhat belatedly, that the promoters dreams were at last to be realised.

The work was of course undertaken as part of the strategy for the eventual re-invasion of Europe on D-Day, but the railway staff and travelling public were naturally ill-informed and instead forced to try and maintain services by means of a bus link calling at all stations. Naturally there was bad feeling as a result and many of those forced to leave the railway were never to return.

Completion of the improvements came in the spring of 1943 after which the railway ran special trains for 24 hours a day, such activities putting a great strain upon the operating staff at all levels.

Despite the pressure, time was found for the occasional prank, such as the time when Winchester-based driver Ton Keogan's locomotive hit an owl whilst working an evening train from Newbury. On arrival at Winchester the dead bird was retrieved and tied to a long chain which operated the gas light in the enginemens' cabin at Bar End. Imagine the consternation of the crew on early shift the next day when in the gloomy darkness they were suddenly confronted with a feathered friend staring them in the face. But despite such occasional releases of tension everyone pulled together and the railway emerged from the years of conflict unscathed.

With a return to peacetime the route assumed its former role, much of the expensive work spent on expansion now being superfluous. Another change in ownership came in 1948 when the GWR was absorbed into the British Railways network, although many of the staff recollected that there was little practical change for them at this time.

▶▲Worthy Down station from the road bridge looking north with the station in the course of transition in autumn 1942. The original platform to the right is in the course of being replaced, with the tracks slewed in preparation. One line, however, is maintained as a through route for works trains and also for a single goods service run daily in each direction. Passenger trains however were suspended, replaced by a bus service that took a tortuous route calling at all stations. Passengers would thus purchase rail tickets in the usual way, although luggage accommodation was strictly limited. Small wonder perhaps that those forced to desert the railway at this time never returned. *British Railways*

▶'Duke' class 4–4–0 No. 3267 *CORNISHMAN* at Winchester Chesil prior to departure for Newbury c.1936. the use of clerestory stock was by now common on less important services. In the left-hand corner a clear impression is gained of the diamond-patterned surface of the down platform. *C.R.L. Coles*

CHAPTER 4

THE ROUTES DESCRIBED

The Main Line

Travelling south from Waterloo it is often the custom of the passenger intending to alight at Winchester to start arranging his effects when passing through Wallers Ash Tunnel, but few spare a thought as to the necessary excavations carried out so that the railway could pass through this particular fold in the Hampshire Downs.

The tunnel itself is some 497 yards long, lined in brick throughout its length and with some 26 refuges for workmen alternately spaced either side. Although cut through porous soil it is surprisingly dry and has been relatively free from incident, apart from that related in the first chapter. But conditions endured by the men during the pioneering days of the railway are far different from today's, so much so that Major General E.W. Pasley was moved to comment upon these at the time of his investigations into the accident of April 1842. At the time he found men working in a 'galley' 30 feet long ,15 feet wide and 7 feet high above the roof and which necessitated packing by hand, the work proceeding without any storing and illuminated by candles. Access was through a hole cut into the roof itself; small wonder perhaps that when accidents occurred they were often with tragic consequences.

But leaving behind the darkness of this cavern, let us return to the railway as it emerges from the tunnel to enter one of the deep chalk cuttings so typical of the London and Southampton line. This particular cutting is straight and true for over half a mile before passing under the roadway leading from Springvale to Wonston. For a short time there is an embankment, providing a view to the east of the urban sprawl of Hookpit and Springvale, an area designated for residential under the 'Homes for Heroes' policy applicable soon after the end of World War I.

After Springvale is another cutting, but only of shallow height before emerging to rolling farmland to the left and an embankment side to the right. It is also possible on the right to discern the former DN & S line running at an angle to, and below the level of the main line. A little further on two parallel arches mark the point of divergence of the former wartime connection from Worthy Down towards Winchester Junction, this latter link being just visible as it climbs up to join the main line. Today the actual site of the line down to the DN & S is marked by a substation providing power for the eletrified line. This building has already stood on the site longer than the railway once passing over it.

Following the cessation of the spur in 1950, the single line was relegated to that of a long siding trailing in from Worthy Down and found a new use for stock storage, mainly vehicles destined for the works at Eastleigh and for which there was no room at Micheldever. Unfortunately after the attention of vandals there was often little left of the vehicles, whilst those undertaking national service at Worthy Down were known occasionally to utilise them for somewhat dubious purposes!

Winchester Junction was of course also the site of the junction with the Alton line which curved in from the left with the signalbox controlling the three lines in the 'V' of the Mid Hants junction. Close to the line at this point was a group of railwaymens cottages, these providing somewhat spartan and isolated accommodation for three families.

Just south of the junction two underbridges are crossed, the first taking the DN & S under the main line and south-east towards Kings Worthy, whilst the second is an occupation roadway leading to nearby Woodhams Farm. The line now continues its course southwards on a embankment and past the site of the intended south connection to Kings Worthy. After a short distance the conifers either side give way to unrestricted views of open farmland, this being altered from the early 1970s by the new bridge carrying the railway over the A34 link road.

Once again the route is due south, the embankment continuing and dissected by another underbridge taking a lane from Three Maids Hill to Springvale. The embankment continues unabated and with the ground falling away all the time, rail level is now some 60 feet above the valley floor, the embankment sides planted with trees to improve stability. With such a depth of earth under the line, understandably the next bridge, Wellhouse Lane, is of a fair length

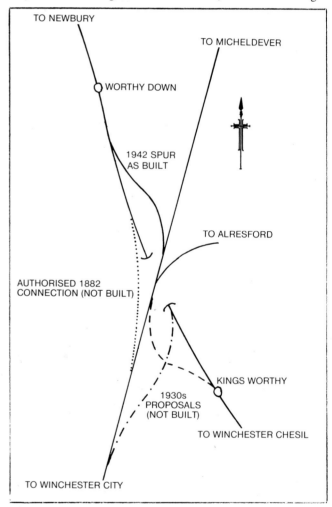

WINCHESTER JUNCTION, ALSO SHOWING PROPOSED CONNECTIONS BETWEEN DN & S AND SR LINES.

A photograph taken from Winchester Junction signal box. A good impression is gained from this of the spur leading off towards Worthy Down. The lines falling through a chalk cutting very apparent. Today the site of the junction is marked by a sub-station feeding the electrified third rail system, whilst Winchester Junction signal box officially closed in 1978, although out of use for some time before this.   *J.L. Farmer*

A driver's eye view approaching Winchester Junction from Itchen Abbas. On the left is a timber platelayers hut used for storage of a small rail-born trolley.   *J.R. Fairman collection*

A delightful study of the railway cottages at Winchester Juncton c. 1905. These wcre built around the time the Mid. Hants line opened to provide accommodation for the signalman at the junction box.
Kings Worthy local History Socety

Fair exchange. Signalman John Brown delivering the tablet to Ernie Salter driver of an Alton train, and receiving in its place a packet of special train notices for Winchester Junction.

J.R. Fairman collection

Diesel units crossing at Winchester Junction with Alton line services. The bracket signal to the left had once sprouted three arms, that missing on the extreme left referring to the connection to Worthy Down. The centre arm still refers to the main line through Walters Ash whilst the right-hand signal will shortly be lowered for the train in the foreground to proceed towards Itchen Abbas.

P.J. Cupper

compared with the formation width at rail level, the narrow arch now utilised by a considerable amount of vehicular traffic.

After this, rolling farmland comes up again to meet the line for a short distance and where for many years a foot crossing existed. Near to here, on the up side, had been the little Worthy signal box, a diminutive structure of four levers, its purpose to break up the section between Winchester Junction and Winchester so allowing for greater line occupancy. In 1932 this signal box was considered redundant and was abolished.

Either side the land once again rises, followed by Park Road overbridge. This like all the other over-bridges in the vicinity is a pleasing mellow brick structure. On the left the 'Baltic Siding' runs parallel with the main line, the wartime platform and Winchester loop signal box long since having disappeared. A further overbridge, this time on a skew angle, carries Andover Road across the line, whilst a separate arch on the left, added in 1883, carried the road over the baltic siding. The extensive siding accommodation once such a feature of Winchester station and mainly added in 1895 would have been visible to the right, a small wooden ground frame controlling the points affording exit to the main route. For many years a shunting engine was retained to operate the yard, its time spent manoeuvering vehicles between the up and down sides as well as occasionally attaching and detaching the odd van from main line services.

Winchester station itself was built in the same basic design originally utilised for most of the stopping places on the London–Southampton line. The extensive rebuilding over the years has removed many of the original features although elsewhere, notably at Micheldever and Southampton Terminus, the structures are little altered. The station has always boasted a good revenue from passengers, commuters travelling to London and students heading for the colleges at Eastleigh and Southampton accounting for much of this traffic. Indeed, those who have had recourse to use the station for any length of time will no doubt recollect the particular drawl of the station announcer, who when disappearing into his office alongside the ticket barrier would announce a '*H*alton train, Itchen Abbas, Alresford, Ropley, Medstead and Halton, change at *H*alton for Bentley, Farnham and Aldershot, Ash Vale', as if the last named place was always an afterthought. Similarly on the down side it would be 'Shawford, Eastleigh, Swaythling, St. Denys, Northam, Southampton Terminus Train', special emphasis put on the last three words, more reminiscent of an auctioneer at a fish market than an announcer on a railway station.

The station also boasted its share of regular VIPs, Lord Mountbatten, for example, being a regular traveller, preferring to drive from Broadlands near Romsey rather than use his local station.

A typical Alton line train of decades past with M7 class 0–4–4T No. 104 on the 2-coach push-pull working. This was the 10.44 a.m. service on 23rd June 1943 as seen looking north from Andover Road bridge with Park Road arch visible in the distance. To the right is the 'Baltic' siding.

F.E. Box

S15 class 4–6–0 No. 513 on a down goods entering the station on 5th April 1943. Such trains often consisted in excess of 60 vehicles and with brakes only on the locomotive and brake van they were a headache to the operating authorities. Provided though that all went normally there was no problem, but such was not the case on Monday evening 22nd August 1960 as reported in the Hampshire Chronicle. ""Rail traffic was held up for several hours outside Winchester City station early on monday evening when two goods trucks loaded with steel girders were derailed during shunting. The main down line from Waterloo was blocked, seriously affecting westbound trains carrying holidaymakers and people travelling to work in Alton were also delayed, as single line traffic was operated."

F.E. Box, courtesy National Railway Museum

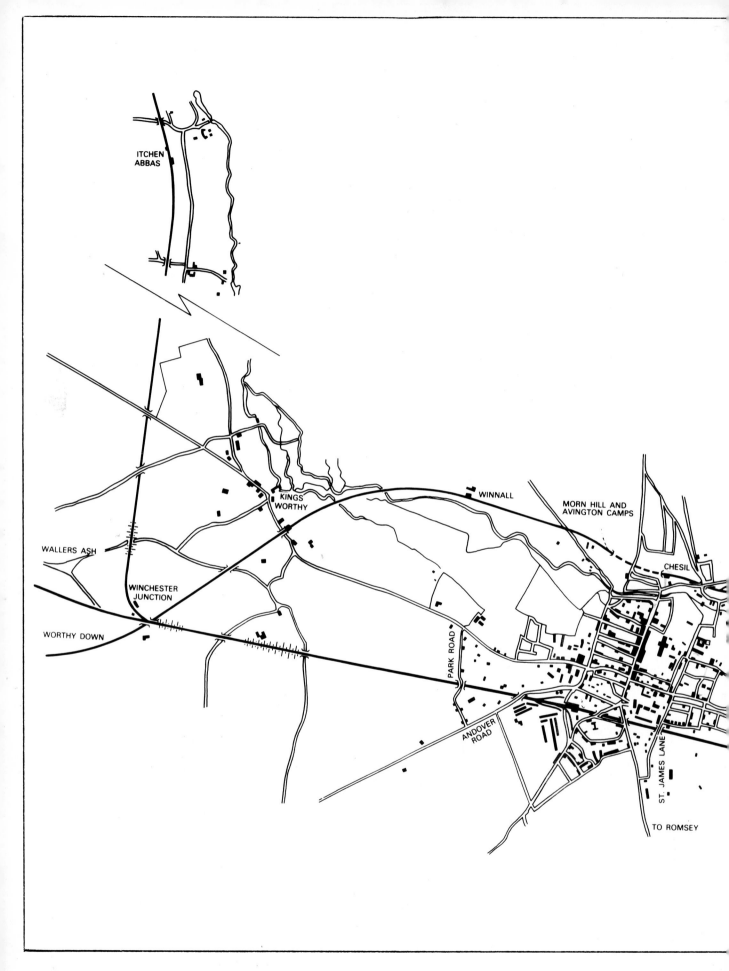

ITCHEN ABBAS

KINGS WORTHY

WINNALL

MORN HILL AND AVINGTON CAMPS

CHESIL

WALLERS ASH

WINCHESTER JUNCTION

WORTHY DOWN

PARK ROAD

ANDOVER ROAD

ST. JAMES LANE

TO ROMSEY

ROUTE DESCRIPTION MAP FOR ALL LINES

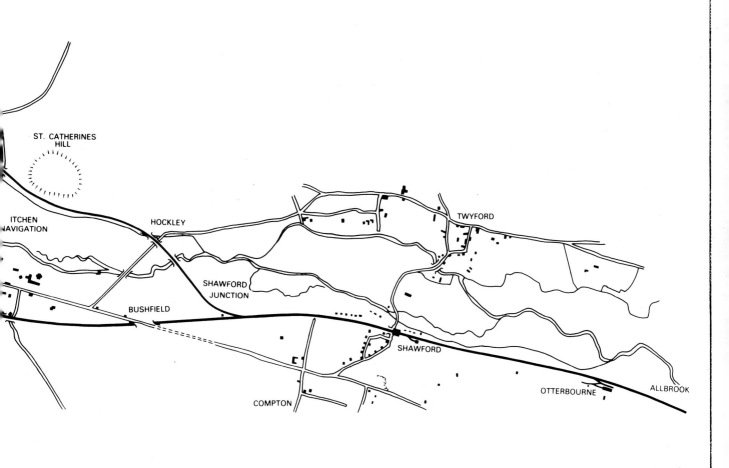

▲ A particularly busy scene on 3rd May 1963 with, on the left Urie S15 No. 30512 with a collection of diesel shunters bound for Eastleigh Works passing sister engine No. 30498 ready to depart with a goods service.

M.J. Fox

▲ A running-in turn from Eastleigh finds 'West Country' class No. 34020 on the main line south of Winchester station with St.James' Lane overbridge in the background, 8th May 1948. The pathway to the left ran alongside the line for some way and was another favourite haunt for loco spotters, especially during steam days.

F.E. Box, courtesy National Railway Museum

The station forecourt on 5th July 1939 taken at the time of the extension to the office and parcels accommodation seen under construction on the left of the view. *F.E. Box, courtesy National Railway Museum*

Transition from steam to electric period, showing the platforms at the southern end of the station being lengthened to accommodate twelve coaches, the anticipated number for the new services. BR Standard class 5 4–6–0 No. 73088 enters the station with a Waterloo service. *Lens of Sutton*

A familiar figure to the regular users of the station in post war years was ticket collector 'Blower' (Arthur Apps) seen here in characteristic pose at the up platform barrier in February 1965. *Rod Hoyle*

Invisible from a train is the underbridge taking Stockbridge Road traffic under the platforms. This structure is a mixture of brick arch and girder construction, due to its extension at the time of the up side yards improvements. Also invisible from the train is the access subway running beneath the track to connect the two platforms.

Leaving the station southwards the cutting sides begin again, the end of the platform being followed by a three arch bridge supporting the Upper High Street after which the cutting continues with a further three arch bridge this time with the busy Romsey Road above. As the cutting sides slowly begin to slope away it is just possible to catch a glimpse of the Peninsular Barracks on the left after which a final bridge, this time a single arch type, signifies the end of the cutting and a resumption once again to embankments.

After passing under St. James Road the next major feature is the small Winchester football ground to the right, immediately after which comes Ranelagh Road underbridge and the areas of St. Cross and Stanmore, to the left and right respectively. Peering almost back on oneself behind the high walls of the houses of Ranelagh Road was of course the site of the siding used in the construction of the Stanmore Estate, the extent of this development now taking in almost the whole of the side of the valley, virtually it seems as far as the horizon. A small public footpath now passes underneath after which comes the single low bridge taking Stanmore Lane under the railway and which continually causes difficulty to the local bus operators.

The land now rises again almost to rail level, with Stanmore School to the right and the pleasantly sounding Whiteshute Lane opposite. This is followed by the only level crossing between London and St. Denys to survive recent times – that of St. Cross which finally closed in 1969. There had been a pathway here from ancient times and this was the route taken when the body of King Rufus was carried from the New Forest to Winchester Cathedral for burial, long before the railway came upon the scene. For many years a wooden signalbox controlled the crossing with a group of small cottages opposite as home to the men in charge.

With the line now entering a shallow cutting there is also the first curvature of any magnitude since Worting (near Basingstoke). St. Cross Tunnel follows, hardly meriting such a title, for at 62 yards in length it is better described as an elongated overbridge. Above it runs the main Winchester–Southampton road at a skew angle and accounting for its size. The undulating nature of the countryside now returns with rapid changes between cutting and embankments as the railway passes under two more overbridges each with farm tracks and then encounters the site of the signal box at

Shawford Junction. The signal box itself was an isolated outpost, approached from another farm track which lead to a bridge just south of the junction and then went up through some woods to the main road. From earliest times the junction was under the control of a South Western man and quite often he would show his allegiance by adopting unnecessary delaying tactics to DN & S trains no doubt to the annoyance of directors and passengers alike.

Shawford Junction is also the starting point for the down relief line, until 1966 accessible only to trains coming from the Newbury direction. There are from now three running lines as far as Eastleigh and these are carried over the curving Winchester by-pass by a structure known locally as the 'Iron Bridge'. In itself it is worthy of a second glance for on the up side are an additional set of brick parapet walls which were provided at the time the bridge was built should an additional track in the northbound direction become necessary.

The lush greenery of the river valley is most obvious from now on although as the line curves gently around to the right this is temporarily lost from view by the sides of yet another shallow cutting. The cutting gives away to a further spell of embankment with Shawford station at its commencement and which, like Winchester, has a road running almost at right angles under the platforms. The station itself has survived remarkably well bearing in mind the stringent economies made during recent years, and whilst the original wooden shelters and canopies have unfortunately been removed, a third platform face on the down relief line allows for a far greater flexibility of working. Part of its success is undoubtedly because of its proximity to what is recognised as a highly desirable residential area, season ticket receipts for the station being very high.

When viewed from certain angles the goods yard at Winchester appeared quite extensive, only later on to be converted into a car park. Here M7 0–4–4T No. 30032 brings in a down 2-coach working off the Alton line and bound for Southampton Terminus. *R.C. Riley*

▶Shawford Junction signal box faced the main line, the 1931 extension is just discernible on the left. *R.C. Riley*

◀St Cross signal box and crossing from the path leading down from Badgers Farm. Below the left-hand end window of the signal box a dark stain indicates where generations of signalmen have emptied their tea pots. The design of signal box was one of several used by the South Western during the latter part of the last century, a similar brick-built example with 'centre pillar' existing for many years at Winchester Junction. *F.E. Box, courtesy National Railway Museum*

From the occupation bridge, Shawford Junction looking north. The main line continues straight ahead with the DN & S on the right. The view was taken before 1943 when the down relief line was extended back from Shawford station to the Newbury branch. When built there had been a crossing loop on the branch itself, of little real use though for trains could always cross on the main line. Accordingly, by 1921, this facility was declared redundant and removed. *Lens of Sutton*

At Shawford station the down loop curved around the platform. Here rebuilt Merchant Navy class No. 35030 *ELDER DEMPSTER LINES* enters the station area during the final weeks of steam.
J.R. Fairman

▲Bulleid-designed Q1 0–6–0 No. 33002 on coaching set No. 816 running e.c.s. on 6th April 1963.
M.J. Fox

Below the embankment to the east of the station is a clear view of that earlier form of transport, the Itchen Navigation. Both road and waterway run basically parallel now almost as far as Allbrook. South of the station, the small goods yard on the west side has for many years been in the hands of a civil engineering contractor. Although the sidings were removed some years ago, the wooden goods shed remains.

Until the introduction of multiple aspect signalling in the area, a connection existed from the down main line into the down relief line at this point, the opposite up relief line terminating in a sand drag almost at the end of the goods yard. It was at this point in the summer of August 1952 that a 'Lord Nelson' class locomotive No. 30854 *Howard of Effingham* overran the signals to finish up on its side at the bottom of the embankment, fortunately without serious injury to either passengers or crew. The resulting operation to recover the locomotive occupied several days and was viewed by numerous spectators from nearby Shawford Down which overlooks the railway and valley at this point. There was even an ice-cream seller in attendance, as watching others labour can indeed be most exhausting!

Four running lines now exist all the way from Shawford to Eastleigh, the quadrupling taking place in 1931 and being part of a scheme originally intended to run all the way from Basingstoke to Southampton. A short cutting follows with a private footbridge spanning the line, before it swings right and into the area geographically known as Otterbourne. The siding of the same name is accessible only off the up relief line and was served twice weekly by the daily Eastleigh and Winchester goods, this being the procedure adopted following the closure of Otterbourne signal box at the time of the lines quadrupling.

The four-track section through Otterbourne and on to Eastleigh was also the last opportunity for drivers of down trains to make up time before reaching Southampton, and the speed of several services rose well into the high eighties and beyond at this point.

With the iron bridge just visible in the background behind the last vehicle, Standard class 5 4–6–0 No. 73085 heads a down inter-regional service near Shawford in the early 1960s.
Tony Molyneaux

An almost new DEMU No. 1110 leaving the station for Eastleigh in 1958. The area around Shawford was fully track-circuited and controlled from neighbouring Shawford Junction, the position of each train shown by means of an illuminated piece of track upon a diagram within the signal box.
Tony Molyneaux

S15 4–6–0 No. 30512 makes an atmospheric passage past the up relief line sand drag en route from Southampton Docks to Feltham on 30th September 1961. Nine years prior to this 'Lord Nelson' class 4–6–0 No. 30854 fully tested this security device.
J. Courtney Haydon

Urie S15 4–6–0 No. 30496 coasts down the easy gradient on the 30th September 1961 with the 9.45 a.m. Feltham to Eastleigh goods.

J. Courtney Haydon

Unrebuilt 'West Country' 4–6–2 No.34007 *WADEBRIDGE* heading south on the down main line just Shawford and with Bowkers private footbridge spanning all four lines just visible.

T. Molyneux

The Newbury Line

Leaving the main line at Shawford Junction, the Newbury line took a curved path leading directly on to the Hockley viaduct, a magnificent brick structure of 31 arches and which since the 1930s has had the Winchester by-pass along one side and so marring the picturesque views to be had of the lush water meadows. It was a joke amongst railway staff to refer to a train leaving the main line at Shawford Junction as, 'running off the timetable onto the calender', such comments being a throw back to the rivalry once existing between the respective owners of the rival lines.

Certainly there was a degree of truth in such comments, for speeds on the DN & S could never match those of the main line and no fault of the engine crews but were caused by the sharp curves and steep gradients often to be found on a cross country route.

BRCW type 3 No. D 6536 runs of the Newbury branch with empty oil tank cars for Fawley Oil Refinery. The two open wagons behind the locomotive were used to separate the power unit from the highly combustible freight. 6th April 1963. *M.J. Fox*

Two well-known railway enthusiasts of recent times discuss their mutual interest in Shawford Junction signal box. On the left is the late Dr. J.L. Farmer, former Medical Officer of Health for Winchester and a life long enthusiast. Indeed, when not engaged on medical matters he could often be found at or near the lines around Winchester. Right is Signalman Bernard Briggs, a man with a wealth of experience in many grades and departments, having commenced his railway service with the locomotive department and then progressed through signalman's, guard's and managerial posts to his present position on the senior staff at Eastleigh. *Bernard Briggs collection*

◄The fireman of 2251 class 0–6–0 No. 2240 picks up the tablet at Shawford Junction as the 2.12 p.m. Eastleigh to Newbury service takes the single line on 27th February 1960.

J. Courtney Haydon

▼A super view of BR class 4 2–6–0 No. 76010 about to take the down relief line at Shawford Junction on 21st March 1963. The 10 m.p.h. speed restriction applied to the hand-over of the single line tablet, although drivers were sometimes known to obey this more in spirit than in practice. To the left of the engine, and boarded over, is the well, used for many years as the water supply to the signal box. It was subsequently condemned as unfit following the discovery of dead rats polluting the bore, water subsequently being delivered in cans, an arrangement that lasted until the box was closed. *J. Courtney Haydon*

With the early morning sun marking out its passage, Standard class 4 4–6–0 No. 75000 heads a Newbury train across Hockley viaduct on 9th January 1960.   *P.H. Swift*

2251 class 0–6–0 No. 2240, a regular performer on the line, and known locally as the 'cuckoo' engine due to the tune from its whistles. The little-used siding to Giffords store is on the left, road access to this a steep climb from nearby Domun Road. In the background is the housing development of Highcliffe, where a chapel was provided for the navvies engaged in the construction of the line. The area of the Bar End yard is now an industrial estate. For many years there had been a Great Western lime works nearby, situated almost on the site of the present Morestead sewage works, little is known of what rail-borne traffic may have been generated. Within the yard there existed, almost up until closure, some rail chairs lettered DNSR.   *E. Best*

After the viaduct came the road bridge at Hockley and a spell where three forms of transport ran together; the Itchen Navigation, railway and Winchester by-pass. Together they pass 'Plague Valley', so called because victims of the black death were buried there. Then past nearby St. Catherine's Hill where once a chapel stood at its peak. Rail and road then parted company with a siding joining the running line to the right, indicating the start of the extensive Bar End yard.

Just past the goods shed there was for many years a small brick built engine shed with a work bench and cupboards along one side and providing basic servicing and stabling needs.

The line was now in a cutting again and swinging slightly to the right before passing under the skew arch of East Hill bridge to emerge alongside Chesil Street before finally entering the station. For many years neither the SR or GWR would acknowledge the existence of each other's line, and would certainly not agree to a proper identity at the stations and it was left to BR to differentiate; Winchester SR taking the additional word 'City' and the former GWR station 'Chesil', itself a connotation of Cheeshill, the original name given to St. Giles' Hill where cheese markets were once held.

The station buildings were on the up or Newbury side, in a design so typical of the GWR and for much of its life it was in a serene and sylvan setting surrounded by conifers and the beauty of St. Giles Hill itself. Overlooking the mellow brickwork of the station was the Station Master's house. This was of similar construction and with an upstairs office so situated that the occupier could survey the comings and goings on the station forecourt at the same time. Tucked away as it was at the lower end of the city, not everyone was even aware of the station's existence, those that do, recalling an individual character and quiet charm which would have been impossible to create amidst the bustle of a main line station environment. One feature of this charm was no doubt the footbridge, setting off the complete site aesthetically, as well as its intended purpose of linking the two platforms. To mount its wooden treads and feel them give slightly underfoot, and then across the top where the worn boards afforded a glimpse of the track far below was to experience a slight tremble inside. Even more frightening was when one could peer down from this lofty perch and see the roaring fire of the engine.

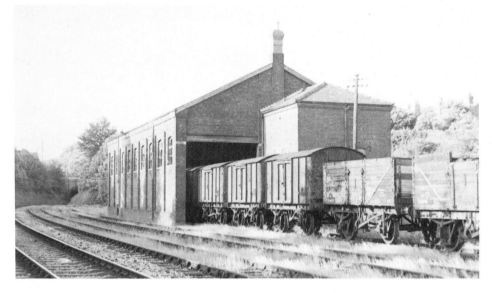

Bar End goods shed with the lines in the yard somewhat overgrown although the single running line is clear. In the background is East hill bridge, the running line at this point relaid with concrete sleepers, later recovered and re-used in sidings at a northern oil refinery.   *E. East*

Bar End engine shed with the siding in the background leading towards the turntable.   *E. Branch*

Leaving the station, the line immediately plunged into the tunnel which is situated on a right-hand curve and varied in length dependent upon which side was measured. This accounted for a 2-yard differential and enabled the track gang to obtain 'tunnel allowance' where previously they had failed to qualify, as the shorter distance was only classed as a bridge under GWR rules!

Following the darkness the line emerged to an equally gloomy cutting after which two overbridges carried the footpath access at the end of Ebden Road and Easton Lane over the railway. Following this the double line gave way to a single track once more, the driver then opening the regulator for the climb past Winnall estate and the adjacent industrial premises. Just before the railway began to swing to the left, a clatter of pointwork indicated the presence of the Winnall siding after which a low 3-arch bridge took the line over the River Itchen. The course was now on an embankment, lasting for only a short distance and affording a panoramic view of the approaching Kings Worthy village to either side.

▲ A post 1948 view of Winchester Chesil as viewed from near East Hill bridge with, left to right, the loading dock, single running line and down siding leading from Bar End. During 1894 plans had been drawn up for an additional siding at this point from the Bar End line across the running line and loading dock siding to terminate near the road in Chesil Street. What its function would have been is unclear and for unknown reasons it was never built.

▼After 1953 Eastleigh-based locomotives began working some trains on the DN & S. To illustrate this, T9 4–4–0 No. 30117 from Eastleigh prepares to depart with the 2.56 p.m. Oxford–Southampton Terminus train on 12th March 1955. *S.C. Nash*

The scene at King's Worthy station on the last day of passenger services, 5th March 1960. This view is taken from the former down platform, disused since 1955.   *J. Courtney Hardon*

►Worthy Down from the air during wartime and clearly showing the rebuilt facilities to advantage. The railway runs north to south to the right of the photograph, its proximity to what was H.M.S. Kestrel clearly apparent. Of particular interest are the two parallel lines south of the road bridge, these are two separate lines one of which leads to the new Winchester Junction spur and the other the usual route to King's Worthy. They merge into one before passing under the road bridge, although clearance exists at this point for a double track.   *Fleet Air Arm Museum*

◄Standard Class '9' 2–10–0 No. 92007 pounding up the 1 in 106 gradient of the DN & S from King's Worthy and about to pass under the main line. The double track formation of the branch is clearly visible in this view, with the disused width for a second track that was never laid occupied by sleepers in the course of relaying. *P.J. Cupper*

▼Sub-ganger George Osman (centre) with two members of the Reading paint gang on the DN & S where it passes under the main line at Winchester Junction. George worked the section of line from King's Worthy to Worthy Down and walked the length daily with his key hammer to check where repairs were necessary as well as to carry out routine maintenance.   *Alack Osman*

Shortly afterwards the line entered the station of the same name. Here the buildings on both sides were of timber and in their last years desperately in need of a repaint. The main building on the up side contained a porters room and passengers approaching from the road below were able to summon the porters' services by means of an electric bell mounted upon the gate-post of the approach path. Despite its shabby appearance, passenger receipts at the station were maintained at a reasonable level up to the cessation of services.

Leaving the station, the Winchester–Kings Worthy road passed beneath, after which the goods yard became visible; for many years dealing primarily in coal. The embankment and climb continued unabated, passing over Springvale Road bridge with the housing development of the same name on the right and open farmland opposite leading to some watercress beds. In the distance could be seen an embankment running left to right indicating the position of the main line, the DN & S passing underneath and then swinging to the right under an occupation bridge within a shallow tree-lined cutting.

As the cutting sides fell away to be replaced by an embankment, the connection from Winchester Junction came into view, together with the parallel brick arches spoken of earlier. The remainder of the distance to Worthy

Down was still on an embankment with the new line running alongside to the right until a clatter of pointwork provided a clue as to the approach to the station. This was entered immediately after an overbridge, the embankment having subsided and given way once more to an undulating landscape.

As with Kings Worthy, the station here was on a falling gradient back towards Winchester, care having to be exercised whenever goods wagons were shunted into position for unloading. Only very basic passenger accommodation was provided in the form of a single island platform with waiting shelter. The signalman was also responsible for the booking office duties in the nearby office although apart from the occasional serviceman's ticket to deal with there was little accounts paperwork. As with all the offices, financial returns had to be prepared daily and submitted via a leather pouch, which also contained used tickets, via a train, to Winchester.

Leaving the station, the camp perimeter fence was visible to the left, whilst opposite there was the usual farmland. With the climb continuing, the line passed under Alresford Drove overbridge, the two lines singling again as the railway entered the deep Christmas Hill cutting towards its next destination at Sutton Scotney.

The Alton Line

Diverging from the main line at Winchester Junction the railway ran towards Itchen Abbas almost due east, to emerge from the junction cutting onto a high embankment overlooking the area of Springvale. In such a manner it crossed the main Springvale Road with the DN & S just visible to the south. But this line was soon lost from view as entering a high cutting the route took the train under Loveden Lane and then shortly afterwards the A33 Winchester–Basingstoke road.

As with the two lines already described the terrain of the Mid Hants line was an accumulation of alternate cuttings and embankments and with little level ground on which the engineer was able to lay his single track. Indeed, for the passenger, the first views of open countryside came as the train approached Martyr Worthy, where southwards it was just possible to catch a glimpse of the River Itchen flowing from its source near Cheriton.

Another cutting was now bisected by a minor road bridge leading to Bridgets Farm after which a spell of embankment carried the train past the parish of Chilland to the right, and if the weather was clear, a distant view could be had of Itchen Wood opposite. The train was now visibly slowing as it entered another cutting swinging gently to the left to emerge at the single platform of Itchen Abbas station.

From Winchester the first three stations on the line, viz Itchen Abbas, Alresford and Ropley were all constructed in the same style, such a move being economic sense to the small company. Itchen Abbass had for some 60 years boasted two platforms, a signal box and a crossing loop. However in 1931 these facilities were reduced to a single platform along with a short line leading off to a diminutive goods yard, for many years the haunt of a solitary van.

Despite its setting, Itchen Abbas was certainly on a par with Shawford with regard to private accommodation nearby, but the station never boasted much in the way of income and was small when compared with its neighbour Alresford. This latter locality was the train's next stop and standing on the tarmac platform it was possible to watch the last coach slowly disappearing from view towards the eventual destination at Alton.

M7 0–4–4T No. 30356 on the 4.10 p.m. Alton–Southampton train at Itchen Abbas on 2nd June 1956. Since 1931 there has been a single platform in use whilst three years earlier, in 1928, the position of stationmaster had been abolished with overall control exercised from neighbouring Alresford.   *J.H. Aston/Lens of Sutton*

▶▲A view up Station Hill towards the City station around the turn of the century with, it is believed, the stationmaster accompanying a visitor. Accommodation for the stationmaster was at first provided in the station buildings, later superceded by a house called 'The Glen' just around the corner at the top left of the picture. Visible as the last building to the top left of Station Hill is the 'South Western' public house, still in existence today and carrying the same name over 60 years after the railway with that title ceased to exist. To supplement the original station building an extension was constructed in brick. By one of the horse-drawn cabs is a drinking fountain and horse watering rough.
Malcolm Snellgrove collection

▶One of Chapman & Co's. carriers vehicles posed outside the station c.1900. The involvement of the North Western Railway at Winchester is unclear. The large clock above the canopy, so familiar a feature of the station, was not provided until shortly before the view was taken, the South Western seemingly reluctant to supply such an obvious facility.
Rodney Youngman collection

CHAPTER 5

THE STATIONS

WINCHESTER

WINCHESTER

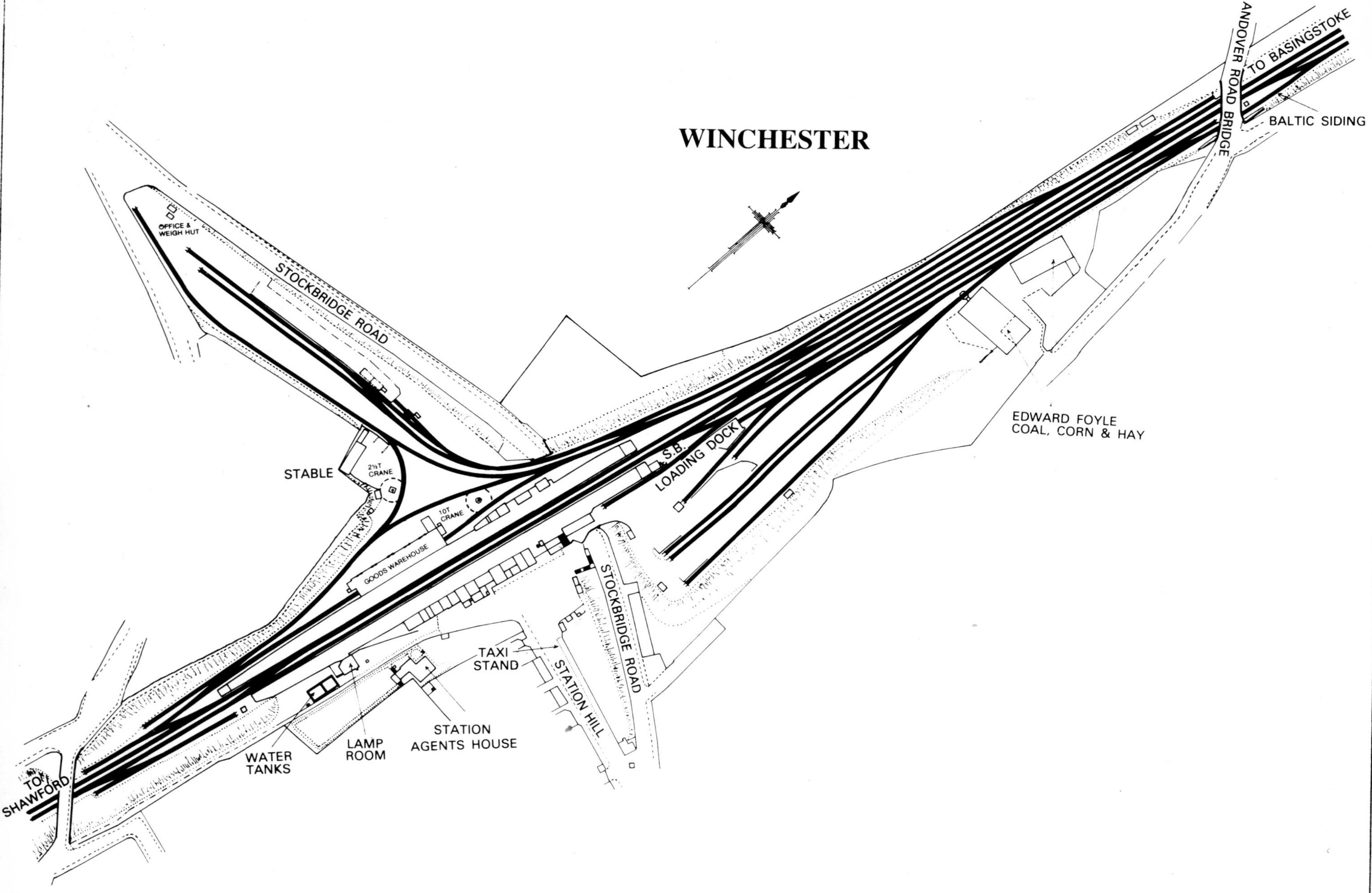

TO BASINGSTOKE

BALTIC SIDING

ANDOVER ROAD BRIDGE

EDWARD FOYLE
COAL, CORN & HAY

S.B.

LOADING DOCK

STOCKBRIDGE ROAD

STATION HILL

TAXI STAND

STATION AGENTS HOUSE

10T CRANE

GOODS WAREHOUSE

LAMP ROOM

STOCKBRIDGE ROAD

2½T CRANE

STABLE

WATER TANKS

OFFICE & WEIGH HUT

TO SHAWFORD

Few views of the station in its early days appear to have survived, this one was taken in 1919 and looks north from Upper High Street bridge. The structure with the sloping roof midway along the righthand embankment is the water tank, columns being supplied at either end of the station. A few years before the photograph was taken a short engine siding had existed at the end of the down platform whilst previous to this there were even wagon turntables leading back towards Station Hill from this end of the site. 60 years later nature has encroached almost as far as the running lines on either side, although otherwise the view is little changed today.
L & GRP, courtesy David & Charles

Schools class 4-4-0 No. 929 *MALVERN* passing through the station with what would appear to be a special working, 20th August 1939. Characteristic of Winchester was the 3-arch bridge at the end of the platform, and which along with the other overbridges beyond gives the station its totally unique appearance. *Author's collection*

A member of the station staff waits for an up train to clear the barrow crossing in 1938. *E. Branch*

▲Shawford for Twyford station with Lord Nelson 4–6–0 No. 30853 *SIR RICHARD GRENVILLE* pounding through with an express for Bournemouth durng 1958.

D. Fereday Glenn

◀Stationmaster 'Spike' Hughes at Winchester c.1948, the post-holders title having been changed over the years from that of Station Superintendent. At the time Mr. Hughes was responsible for a staff of approximately 60, consisting 9 clerks, 3 signalmen, 3 parcels clerks, 2 shunters, 4 ticket collectors, 7 platform porters, 2 foremen, 2 enginemen, 9 PW staff, 11 goods checkers and porters and 7 motor drivers. The number of staff is a clear indication as to the amount of traffic handled. Coverage was over a 24 hour period for the signalmen, although the goods side only worked 8 a.m.–5 p.m. The station was open a full 24 hours but in the quiet hours between 2 a.m. and 4 a.m. only one platform porter would be on duty. The porters were also responsible for cleaning and trimming the signal lamps, these being serviced in the lamp hut at the end of the down platform. In addition to dealing with incoming and outgoing goods, the parcels office doubled as a lost property and train enquiry bureau, as well as housing the telephone exchange together with a battery of external phones. All of these were encased in a metal shield, supposed protection against all raids and earning the local nickname 'badgers hole'. Older staff recalled the single needle telegraph instrument as once the only means of outside communication. World War II saw the number of staff maintained but with several replaced by women. They were not however, permitted to work full night shift alone and so the remaining men performed almost permanent 12 hour duty.

F.E. Box, courtesy National Railway Museum

▲In connection with the evacuation of troops from Dunkirk, an unknown quantity of special trains were run to move soldiers to various camps. This line of commandeered buses is in Station Hill awaiting the arrival of one such train. *E. Branch*

▼An example of a private owner wagon used at the station. *HMRS*

One of the ubiquitous B4 class 0–4–0 tank engines, this one, No. 102 *GRANVILLE*, is in the course of shunting on the down side on 10th September 1948. Viewed from left to right the main lines are Nos. 3 & 4, the small wooden ground frame released from the signal box and controlled the points affording access to the up side yard. Behind this are the rear of the houses in Brassey Road, the skyline still recognisable today although with the addition of the Police Headquarters topping nearby West Hill.

F.E. Box, courtesy National Railway Museum

B4 No. 83 poses during shunting operations. Note the tarpaulin cover in the cab erected to prevent the cross winds blowing through. 8th May 1943.

F.E. Box, courtesy
National Railway Museum

Within the up side yard a corrugated shed provided a degree of protection for the shunting engine, the last two regular steam shunters being Nos. 30096 and 30102. Each locomotive would remain in use for approximately one week after which there was a slow run to Eastleigh for boiler washout and servicing. Nearby was a small coaling stage and ash bin, these being provided during 1919 at an estimated cost of £25.

J. Courtney Haydon

No. 30093 outside the engine shed, which is now partly playing host to a couple of bicycles. Although it is not confirmed, the locomotive always appeared to face north necessitating a bunker first journey to Eastleigh.   *R.C. Riley*

As well as shunting the yards, the station pilot was also charged with the task of attaching and detaching vehicles to trains as required. A horsebox is seen here being added to the rear of a Western Region DMU on 1st July 1961. Apart from horses, pigeons were a regular traffic, basket-loads of birds being received for releasing to their home lofts. Just visible to the extreme right of the engine, on the opposite platform, is one of the wind breaks protecting passengers along the length of the up platform. *P.J. Cupper*

For much of the time the engine spent its day pushing wagons into the various sidings in the up side yard. Here No. 30093 no doubt attempts to cause little as possible smoke damage to a neighbours washing! *R.C. Riley*

With just two other pieces of rolling stock in view, Q1 0–6–0 No. 33019 trundles through with an engineers train bound for Redbridge.
R.C. Riley

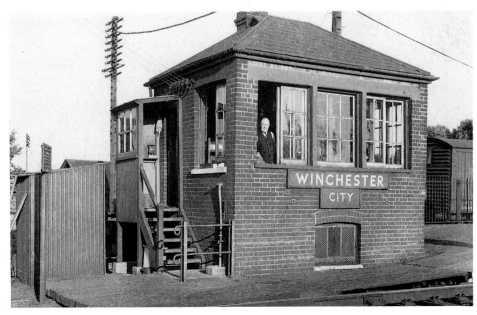

The old brick signal box at Winchester situated at the north end of the up platform and replaced in 1960. Signalman Bill Corps is visible.
Lens of Sutton

Busy times at the City station with rebuilt 'Merchant Navy' No. 35027 *PORT LINE* on the 13-coach up 'Royal Wessex' overtaking S15 4–6–0 No. 30838 shunting in the up side yard, 5th May 1962. *P.J. Cupper*

Hall 4–6–0 No. 4960 *PYLE HALL* approaches with a Reading–Southampton local service. *R.C. Riley*

▲The crew of rebuilt 'West Country' class No. 34008 *PADSTOW* take the opportunity to replenish the tender in February 1965.   *Rod Hoyle*

►Young admirers watch an exhausted-looking fireman aboard No. 34095 *BRENTOR* in March 1965. *Ron Hoyle*

Parcels and newspaper workings were a familiar sight on the main line for decades, with here standard class 4 2–6–0 76033 leaving the down yard for Eastleigh. The replacement signal box, opened in 1960 was destined to have a working life of exactly six years, although it still survives as office accommodation. *Tony Molyneux*

An unusual sight at the City station with Britannia class pacific No. 70014 *IRON DUKE* heading the 1.15 p.m. Bournemouth West–Waterloo service on 17th May 1951. This loco together with 70004 *William Shakespeare* were allocated to Stewart's Lane depot (73A) for the Golden Arrow service and other boat trains. The signal is of interest due to the amount of spare post above the arm. Whether this was a new post or the arm was later resited is unclear, for certainly in later years the anomaly was corrected. *L. Elsey*

▲Modern Winchester as an unidentified class 47/4 draws to a halt with the 09.40 Poole–Newcastle during 1983.   *D. Fereday Glenn*

◀The replacement for the B4 tanks, 204 h.p. Drewry 0–6–0 diesel mechanical shunter No. D 2274 at Winchester in May 1965.   *Rod Hoyle*

SHAWFORD

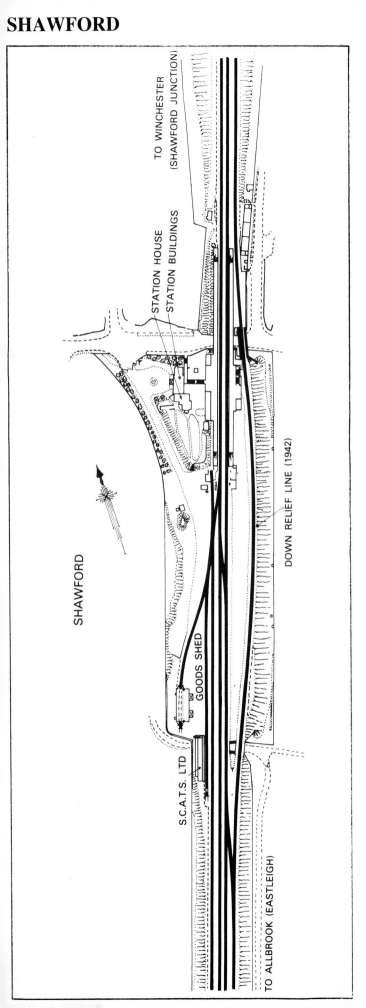

SHAWFORD

TO WINCHESTER (SHAWFORD JUNCTION)

STATION HOUSE
STATION BUILDINGS

DOWN RELIEF LINE (1942)

GOODS SHED

S.C.A.T.S. LTD

TO ALLBROOK (EASTLEIGH)

◄Fred Capon, former Shawford signalman, and shown here at the start of his railway career just after World War I. Fred served in many boxes around the Eastleigh area retiring as District Inspector responsible for a large area. He was a railwayman in the finest sense of the word.

Mrs. Capon collection

►Taken from the north, a view of Shawford station looking towards Eastleigh. over the years standard SR concrete fittings have replaced the timbered platforms. *Lens of Sutton*

►Shawford pre-1931 with the signal box extant. The station is probably little altered from its opening, the wooden buildings at either end of the canopies of particular interest. Their function has yet to be discovered, although possibly they were for parcels or porters offices.*Mrs. Capon collection*

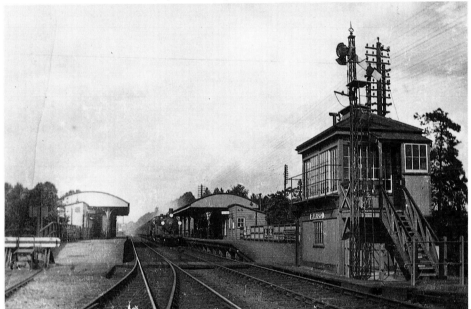

◄The guard prepares to flag away his relatively new DEMU train from Shawford in 1963. *J.R. Fairman*

►Adams 0–6–0 No. 30566 on the down relief line just south of Shawford complete with suitable inscription. The train is the daily transfer freight working from Bar End to Eastleigh and will have served Otterbourne siding in the up direction. *Les Elsey*

With the road set from main line to relief, standard class 4 4–6–0 No. 75074 slowly passes through Shawford destined for Eastleigh.

Tony Molyneaux

2251 class 0–6–0 No. 3210 on a Newbury train passes the station goods yard on 21st June 1958. By this time there was little freight traffic at the station and the sidings were removed shortly afterwards. The wooden platform and shed was used by the PW gang as a base for their trolley.

D. Fereday Glenn

4300 class 2–6–0 No. 6329 on a Southampton service from the Newbury line takes the down relief line around the back of Shawford station. As there was no platform on this line at this time the signalman at Shawford Junction had to be careful to route those trains due to call at the station onto the main line. But mistakes did occur, fortunately not too often.

Lens of Sutton

With the fireman no doubt working hard, T14 4–6–0 No. 30461 blasts through the station with an up fitted freight from Southampton Docks on 5th March 1950.

B.M. Barber

▲Just south of the station there was, up until 1966, a connection from the down main to the down relief line. King Arthur class 4–6–0 No. 30792 *SIR HERVIS DE REVEL* heads north on an up express past the place in question. *Tony Molyneaux*

◀Shawford station signalbox opened in 1982 and closed in 1931. Contemporary reports suggest that there may have been a signalbox in the area sometime after 1870 called Twyford. This was moved when the station was built and renamed as shown above. Signalling records, however, are very scarce and, as with nearby Otterbourne signalbox, other information has not come to light.

Mrs. Capon Collection

WINCHESTER CHESIL

Chesil station as seen from the approach road and giving the appearance of a country railway station. It was at this time in need of a repaint, which was destined not to take place.

Rev D Littlefair

The Great Divide, Chesil Tunnel, some ¼ mile in length, took the railway under the mass of St. Giles, or as it is sometimes referred to, Magdalen Hill. Just inside the tunnel up until 1943 the two lines became one, extreme care having to be exercised when shunting was carried out at this end of the station. The two signals are starting signals for up trains from either platform with a shunt arm beneath (signified by the letter 'S' on the arm itself). What purpose the starter served at the end of the down platform is unclear and has been the subject of much debate, for as far as can be ascertained no trains were ever scheduled to head northwards from this platform.

Malcolm Snellgrove collection

A delightful study of Duke class 4–4–0 No. 3279 *RIVER FAL* after arrival at Winchester from Newbury with a typical train of the 1930s. The engine will shortly be coming off the train and run to Bar End for servicing whilst a Southern locomotive will then take over for the remainder of the run down to Southampton. Characteristic for the period is the well tendered station garden, several of the DN & S line stations being regular winners in the annual station gardens competition.

H.N. Sheppard

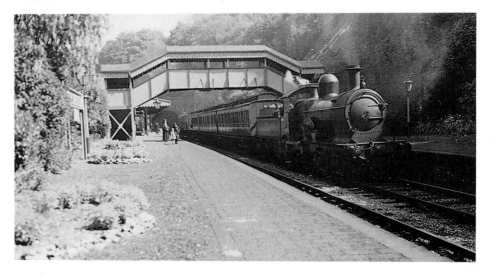

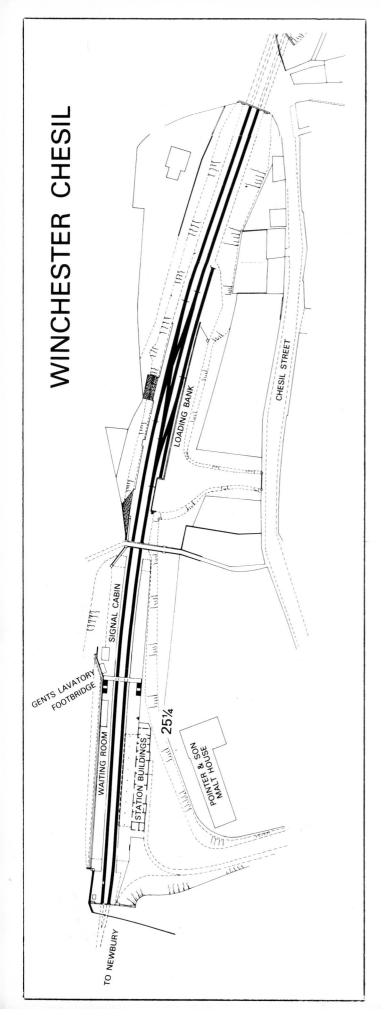

WINCHESTER CHESIL

TO NEWBURY

GENTS LAVATORY
FOOTBRIDGE
WAITING ROOM
STATION BUILDINGS
SIGNAL CABIN
LOADING BANK
CHESIL STREET
POINTER & SON MALT HOUSE

25¼

The local carrier outside the station.
Mr. and Mrs. A Dowlland Collection

Arthur Wellstood (on the right) and an unidentified member of staff at the end of Chesil station building c.1925.   *T. Wellstood*

Just one week before closure, 2251 class 0–6–0 No. 2240 emerges from the tunnel with the 9.07 a.m. Newbury–Eastleigh service on 27th February 1960.
J. Courtney Haydon

The 2251 class were common visitors to the line, although example No. 2200 was not so often seen. Here she heads a down Bar End freight through the station, nearing the end of the journey.
Authors' collection

No more trains and just a few weeks before the scrap merchants moved in. Chesil signalbox and signals August 1966.
J. Courtney Haydon

In almost new condition, the signal box in power signalling days. The man outside thought to be signalman W. Tyrell.
Lens of Sutton

An extremely interesting view taken late 1922 or early 1923 at Winchester Chesil and showing the old and new signal boxes together. This was the time of changeover from mechanical to an experimental form of route setting signalling which required the replacement of the old platform box.
J. D. Francis collection

Just to the south of Chesil station the single line recommenced, the line on the right leading to Bar End yard 2-6-0 No. 6313 leaves the station on 27th February 1960 with the 12.25 p.m. Newbury–Eastleigh service.

J. Courtney Haydon

For a period during the summers of 1959, 1960 and 1961 the saturdays only Southampton–Winchester diesel service was diverted to Chesil and so reduced congestion at the Southern station. Unit 1104 is shown here on the down side in the course of running round. Just visible by the platform trolley on the opposite platform is one of the travelling safes, at the time used for movement of takings from Chesil station.

Hampshire Chronicle

4300 class 2–6–0 No. 7327 awaiting the 'right away' from Winchester Chesil for Newbury on 6th February 1960, a few weeks before closure.

P.J. Cupper

KINGS WORTHY

KING'S WORTHY

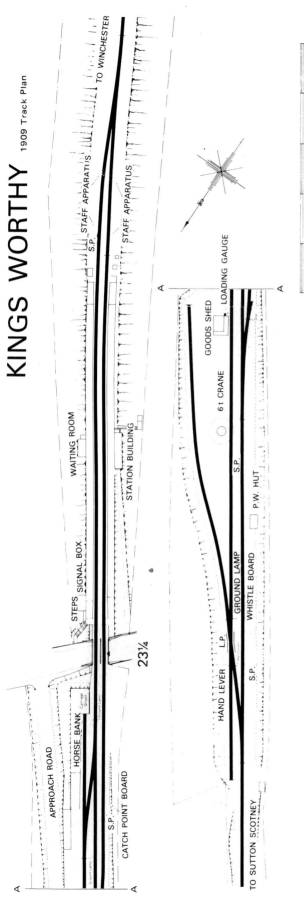

1909 Track Plan

TO WINCHESTER

S.P. STAFF APPARATUS

STAFF APPARATUS

S.P.

LOADING GAUGE

GOODS SHED

6 t CRANE

WAITING ROOM

STATION BUILDING

SIGNAL BOX

STEPS

HORSE BANK

APPROACH ROAD

S.P.

CATCH POINT BOARD

23¼

HAND LEVER

L.P.

GROUND LAMP

WHISTLE BOARD

S.P.

P.W. HUT

S.P.

TO SUTTON SCOTNEY

A — A

CHAINS

Signalman Arthur Watts in the four-foot at Kings Worthy. The signal box here was physically moved in 1942 to the new site shown; this was in connection with the extension of the passing loop. A brick lower shell was also added as a degree of protection against air raids.   *A. Watts collection*

For many years there were two coal merchants at Kings Worthy, Messrs Snow and Bryer Ash, both possessing their own railway wagons. Bryer Ash also had use of an old wooden hut at the approach to the station yard giving their address as 'GWR Station yard, Kings Worthy'. The hut is shown here decorated for the coronation celebrations of 1953.   *A. Watts collection*

A recently discovered postcard depicting the station around the time of opening in February 1909. The view is particularly notable as it is looking south, a prospect seemingly ignored by photographers over the years. the train shown consists of a GWR 0–6–0 goods engine and a brake van originating from Bar End yard, the reason for the working being uncertain. The goods facilities were not officially open when the photograph was taken (being delayed until April that year) and it is just possible that the train was run in connection with the work in progress. The postmark bears a date of 19th February and was sent by one of the station staff, a Mr. Stowell, to his mother (he is with the guard leaning out of the brake van). On the down loop can be seen inside keyed rail with DN & S pattern chairs indicating this was the former running line prior to the station's existence.

C.E.S. Beloe, Author's collection

'Duke' class 4–4–0 No. 3254 *CORNUBIA* on a Winchester service at Kings Worthy in 1934. By this time the platform edges had been refixed with sleepers and an old rail bolted across the front edge to afford stability. 'Tilley' lamps have also been provided using pressurised paraffin vapour and attached to a pulley to be wound up to the top of the post as required.

H.N. Shephard

During 1957 an enterprising BR management resurrected the record breaker *CITY OF TRURO* and restored her to service for working special trains. When not so employed she was based at Didcot working the 12.42 p.m. to Southampton, returning with the 4.58 p.m. service. This latter train called at Eastleigh to collect many of the workers from the nearby depot, and so perhaps to show what Swindon could do. Here City of Truro is seen leaving Kings Worthy. By this time only one platform was in use and today the whole site is taken up by the A34 trunk road.

G. Siviour

The up side buildings, by this time looking as if collapse is imminent! To the left the small wooden hut is the former ground frame relocated on the platform in 1942. *J. Courtney Haydon*

Coal deliveries from Kings Worthy had, in early times, been undertaken by horse and cart although with the passage of years the motor lorry came upon the scene. Here a Morris commercial is in the station yard Kings Worthy. *A. Watts collection*

A Portsmouth–Birmingham train near Winchester being hauled by 4300 class 2–6–0 No. 4395.

WORTHY DOWN

WORTHY DOWN
1943 Track Plan

TO KINGS WORTHY

P.W. HUT

RACECOURSE BRIDGE

Signal Box

Coal

BOOKING AND PARCELS OFFICE

30 cwt CRANE

STORE   SHELTER

A

A

A

A

TO SUTTON SCOTNEY

PETROL PUMPS   STORAGE TANKS

0   1   2   3   4   5   CHAINS

The classic view of Worthy Down with platelayers hut, signal box and booking office to the right and the solitary shelter on the island platform. Little is known of the wartime rail traffic handled here other than aviation fuel, but army personnel certainly used the railway. It would be interesting to ascertain if munitions were ever handled and if so how they were transported to the bomb dumps north of the site. It has been suggested a narrow gauge railway may have existed for this purpose, although no evidence in support of this has so far been uncovered.

Lens of Sutton

Signalman 'Knobby' Bryant walks back towards his signal box after exchanging the single line token with the fireman of T9 4-4-0 No. 30707 working a Didcot–Southampton service.

F. Siviour

ITCHEN ABBAS

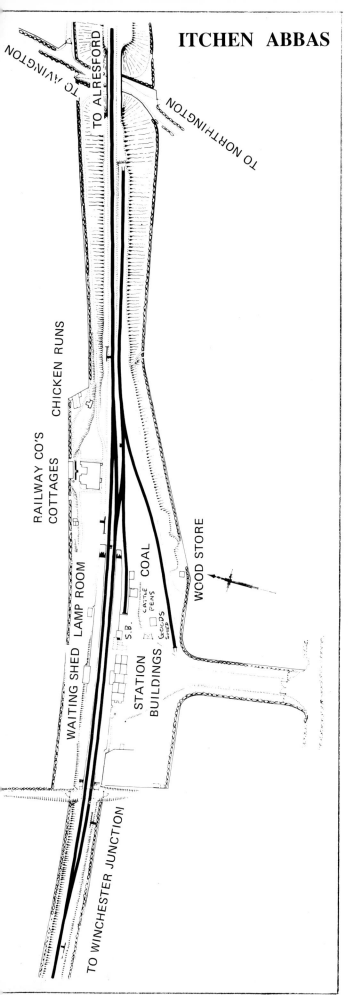

TO AVINGTON

TO ALRESFORD

TO NORTHINGTON

RAILWAY CO'S COTTAGES

CHICKEN RUNS

WAITING SHED

LAMP ROOM

STATION BUILDINGS

S.B.

CATTLE PENS

COAL

GOODS SHED

WOOD STORE

TO WINCHESTER JUNCTION

Itchen Abbas in the early years of the century and no doubt little altered since opening. The stationmaster on the left of the platform may well be Mr. H.J. Delia who was in charge of what was classed as a 'Class 5' station, and earning the salary of £200 p.a. Some years earlier the redoubtable Samuel Fay had started his railway career at Itchen Abbas as a junior clerk; he later rose to high office on the South Western and then to General Manager of the M & SWJ line. He finally became GM of the Great Central Railway and was knighted in 1912.
Malcolm Snellgrove collection

Itchen Abbas station approach and the delightful ivy clad building, home to a member of staff. The design of building was perpetuated at both Alresford and Ropley. *Lens of Sutton*

BRCW type 3 No. D 6585 on the up platform at Winchester with a local working.

Ian Shawyer Collection

For a time after their relegation from front-line duties on the Western Region, the class 42 'Warship' diesel hydraulics found employment on north–south inter-regional trains. One of these is seen cautiously passing Winchester Junction on its way south at a time when an engineers possession rendered it impossible to lower the home signal.

John Farman

CHAPTER 6
THE DECADES OF CHANGE

Nationalisation

Other than locomotives, rolling stock and staff uniforms displaying the BR insignia, the impact of nationalisation had little effect upon the running of the railways locally and this climate was to continue until April 1950 when regional boundary changes were put into effect. From those changes it was decided that the WR, in return for losing control of its mid-England operations, would take over the SR lines west of Exeter, whilst the SR would have control of everything geographically south of the former Berks and Hants line through Reading, Newbury and Savernake. The DN & S from Newbury thus came under the direct supervision of Waterloo for the first time. To many of the traffic and permanent way department staff this was a move recalled as having a far greater impact than the nationalisation of two years earlier. Certainly, in many ways, it made sense but in other respects a lifetime's dealings and practices had to alter overnight. Understandably there was resentment from some quarters.

On the locomotive side, SR engines were used on turns from Eastleigh, their crews first learning the road with the assistance of the Winchester Chesil men. Indeed, it was to result in Didcot and Eastleigh engines working turn and turn about on trains up to the closure. This policy itself was not without humour, as on occasions when Eastleigh men left an SR engine on shed at Didcot and went for their meal break with their steed blocking one of the exit points. They would be traced by a harassed foreman who in no uncertain terms instructed them to '****** move that ****** engine, none of my men will touch it'!

With the Newbury line now under SR control little time was wasted in painting everything in their standard colours of green and yellow, which the author at least thought did not somehow fit in with the GWR structures. But from 1953 change began to gather pace with the Chesil station master being withdrawn and both stations now under the authority of the City man. Then in the spring of 1953 the engine shed

at Bar End was closed which meant that no longer would passengers be subjected to the delay of engine changing on both up and down workings.

Modernisation

Elsewhere on the railways the 1955 modernisation plan promised to upgrade the national network and abolish steam traction, modern technology to play its part in all departments. But many of the staff were more than a bit cynical about the scheme because of the promises made with nationalisation and which still had to be fulfilled. But of one thing there could be little doubt, the system was in desperate need of overhaul. Take for example the Bournemouth line trains, every weekend packed to capacity with passengers standing in the corridors and brake vans. This illustrated that whilst the relaxed travel restrictions and freedom from petrol rationing had made everyone eager to travel, not all had the resources to afford their own private transport.

With the staff still pondering as to their future the first major signs of change came with the removal of crossing loop facilities from Kings Worthy in 1955 as well as two other locations between that point and Newbury. The facilities of the DN & S were seen as being too elaborate and expensive to maintain now that the route was restored to its pre-war role of a sleepy cross-country branch.

Two years later, in 1957, came the first 'Hampshire' Diesel Electric Multiple Units designed to supersede steam on many of the branch line and secondary services within the county. The services began amidst a blaze of publicity and whilst today one may shudder at the thought of travelling in what are noisy and rough riding machines, it must be recalled that for their time they presented a modern, clean and welcome change from the often antiquated stock previously used on some of the services they replaced. In this way the Southampton–Alton, Southampton–Reading and Southampton–Winchester services were to benefit. Surprisingly no diesel service was

The crew of M7 0-4-4T No. 30029 collect the single line tablet from the Shawford Junction signalman whilst on the 8.50 a.m. empty stock from Eastleigh to Winchester Chesil. This will then form the 12.10 p.m. Saturdays only service form Chesil to Southampton Central. *J.L. Farmer*

suggested for the DN & S for the cost of a diesel service was estimated to be double that of receipts prevailing on the line at the time.

Instead, so far as the DN & S was concerned, a third of the service, or two trains each way daily, were withdrawn in June 1958 and it seemed from this that the final future of the line was now determined.

Based upon the word 'economy' these cuts were nothing but necessary, although not attempting to re-time the remaining services to reduce in particular the five hour gap between up services is open to question. Likewise the starting of a Newbury train from Shawford and not Eastleigh or Southampton, particularly as the service ran empty and unavailable to passengers before reaching its starting point, must be highly questionable. Accordingly, passengers for Newbury were faced with the prospect of either rising early, an impossible task if living outside Winchester where no suitably timed bus service into the city existed, or using the bus for the whole journey, this latter action taking a time of almost two hours to complete, allied to numerous detours around the many villages and hamlets along route.

But such changes had not gone unnoticed, for the local press were quick to point out things like, 'Your last chance to travel on a Hampshire Railway' and, 'Lights out on the Winchester–Newbury line', just two of the headlines used. What is perhaps more surprising is the time it took for the railway to eventually close, notices not being posted until the summer of 1959 to take effect from Monday 7th March 1960.

Traffic on the main line and Alton branch were however faring somewhat better with receipts holding up well against an increase in road competition. But even so moves were afoot in the Beeching plan of 1963 to reshape the national railway network to a size more akin to the needs of the day. Beeching dealt solely on the basis of lines and services, the motive power aspects having already having been covered by the previous 1955 modernisation plan. But Beeching did feel there was room for improvement in the area of seasonal traffic peaks particularly in summertime and at Christmas because stock used for these services found little gainful employment for the remainder of the year. The same could also be said of commuter services generally, but here in Hampshire at least these were mainly concerned with the transport of businessmen to and from the capital.

By 1964 the main line services through Winchester were

◄DEMU 1108, one of the new 'Hampshire' diesels on the up side at Winchester in 1957. When first introduced these were 2-coach sets, an extra vehicle added to most of the units as demand increased. On the Alton line services, however, a 3-coach set was often a struggle on the severe climb either side of Medstead and Four Marks.   *Lens of Sutton*

▼The prestige train of the Bournemouth line was without doubt the 'Bournemouth Belle' introduced in 1931 and finally withdrawn with electrification in 1967. Here rebuilt Merchant Navy 4–6–2 No. 35028 *Clan Line* (now preserved) heads the down service just south of Wallers Ash tunnel on 20th February 1960.   *Tony Molyneaux*

beginning to be affected by the run-down condition of the steam locomotives and at this time no final decision had been reached as to the introduction of electric or diesel traction to take over. But eventually the choice was made and full third rail electrification was promised to Bournemouth by the end of 1966 with push-pull units in 8 or 12-coach formations on express services.

Ominously missing from the plans was any mention of the Alton branch, the Beeching report having proposed this for closure as being unnecessary and uneconomic. Not surprisingly such a statement evoked a torrent of enraged public opinion. A series of public meetings and petitions were arranged with the intention of securing the route on the basis of it being in a 'developing area' and also the considerable amount of traffic carried. But to be fair much of the patronage was in the form of school children and students who of course travel during term times only, and with Beeching dedicated to reduce such peaks wherever possible the future was far from certain, especially when in other parts of the country retention of a railway on the grounds of hardship to children during term time was deemed insufficient.

Meanwhile the DN & S was closed to through freight workings as from 9th August 1964, the tanker trains from Fawley now being routed via Basingstoke and Reading. This left the connection from Shawford Junction to Bar End, served at first on a daily basis and then declining to a twice weekly transfer working from Eastleigh.

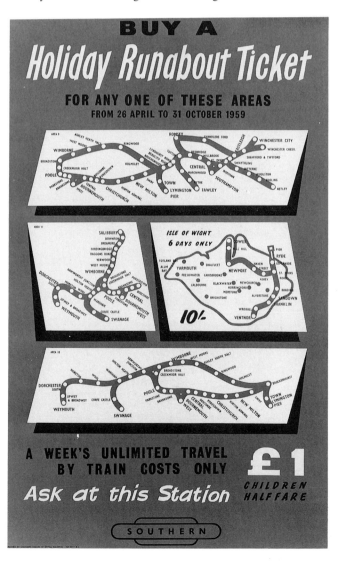

Electrification

Under electrification of the Bournemouth line an anticipated increase of 100% in the number of passengers travelling was confidently forecast for Winchester. The corresponding figures for Basingstoke and Southampton quoted as 150% and 50% respectively. How such conclusions were drawn is unclear, possibly something to do with the Hampshire County Council forecasts for regional development, but more likely on the basis of a series of surveys carried out in which all passengers were invited to participate. Many and varied were the questions asked: "How often do you travel? Are you likely to use the train more when the service is faster?" etc. Of course a lot of these research facilities were undertaken with the commuter in mind, those with season tickets at times invited to travel in a special observation saloon from which the progress of electrification could be monitored. Partly this was done to explain the inherent delays caused by the installation of conductor rail, multiple aspect signalling and the like. The signalling in the Winchester area now came under the control of a new power signal box at Eastleigh, the changeover taking place one windswept night in November 1966. With the closure of the local signal boxes, St. Cross level crossing was provided with a footbridge and the gates reduced to 'occupation' status, a key given to those regular users. At Winchester Junction though the old signal box was retained and still worked in conjunction with Alresford on the Alton line, electrically released from Eastleigh panel when needed. But despite the alterations to trackwork and signalling being almost ready for the new form of traction in late 1966, the stock was not and so the electric service was postponed first to June and finally to July 1967.

Bar End was unaffected by such moves for it had closed in the spring of 1966, the down relief line at Shawford Junction being slewed into the down main line and so forming a new connection.

But it was not all a matter of contraction, for at Shawford a platform was provided for the first time on the down relief line and at Winchester the platforms were extended at the south end to take 12-coach trains. Locally too, a steel erecting firm with premises at Winnall attempted to negotiate for the retention of the DN & S for transport of their products on the basis of a long siding but unfortunately it came to nothing.

The new electric service finally started on Monday 10th July 1967, the main line being served by a fast and semi-fast service to London and Southampton (although the fast service did not call at Winchester) whilst there was also a stopping train. Each ran at the same minutes past the hour throughout most of the day, so certainly the confused timetables of years gone by had at last been superseded. Additionally there were the inter-regional trains, Alton line trains and a daily one each way non stop service from Winchester to Waterloo.

The new service of main line trains was of course vastly different from anything previously seen and accordingly well received. Whether rise in passenger receipts agreed with the forecasts is uncertain but what is known is that for the first time there would shortly be a real challenge to rail supremacy in the form of a comprehensive road building plan for the county.

One of the two posters used for the 1959 advertising of the Holiday Runabout Ticket promotion. Excellent value a only £1 and allowing for unlimited travel within the stipulated areas. Ominously missing from either poster was any ticket covering the DN & S or Alton lines, both still open at the time.   *British Rail*

The first of these, the Otterbourne and Chandler's Ford by-pass, enabled traffic to travel from Winchester to South-ampton in a matter of minutes, avoiding the seemingly endless delays through Winchester Road at Chandler's Ford. Unfortunately the planners failed to realise that the new road would cause severe congestion at either end in the Avenue (Southampton) and St. Cross Road (Winchester).

More of a problem perhaps, was road borne freight traffic and resolved by the building of the Kings Worthy link, a 2-mile dual carriageway linking the northern end of the Winchester by-pass with the A34 at Three Maids Hill and routed for part of its course along the track bed of the former DN & S line. (A connection between the A33 and A34 had been predicted for some time. If the railway remained open the course of the new road would have taken it over the line near to Kings Worthy station, but such proposals never received high level consideration). When completed the road was to remove valuable freight from the railway, a consequence of which was the gradual closure of wayside goods yards, that at Winchester included, as the railway proved unable to compete in a way their customers demanded.

◄Replacement for steam, 4 Vep set No. 7753 on a stopping Waterloo to Bournemouth service entering Winchester September 1985. These units are in use throughout the SR system on semi-fast workings.   *Ian Shawyer*

▼As first introduced into service on 7th July 1967, the Rep and TC units were painted all over blue although this was soon altered to blue and grey. Shortly after the start of the electric service, 4 TC No. 428 leads a Waterloo–Bournemouth semi-fast service into Winchester Station in the summer of 1967.   *Hampshire Chronicle*

An empty tank car train destined for Fawley rolls down the grade through Christmas Hill cutting and towards Worthy Down. Near here was the site of the former Winchester racecourse apparent on early maps and out of use by about 1900.　　　*P.H. Swift*

From the slopes of St. Catherines Hill the northbound 'Solent Freighter' runs alongside the Winchester by-pass on 17th May 1964. The bridge arch just visible to the extreme left shows the position of the original railway prior to the construction of the Winchester by-pass. The railway now having been closed for several years yet still at this point the road retains its narrow width.　　　*P.H. Swift*

Transition from steam. Multi-aspect signalling is ready to take over from the old semaphore equipment and conductor rails are in place as a BRCW type 3 (later class 33) in original green livery arrives on a down express.　　　*J.R. Fairman*

Class 50 No. 50017 *Royal Oak* in revised blue livery with the diverted 12.38 Waterloo–Exeter St. David's on 16th March 1985.   *Chris Wilson*

Class 47/4 No. 47625 *CITY OF TRURO* in with the 08.58 Manchester Piccadilly–Poole also on 16th March 1985.   *Chris Wilson*

The Alton Line Succumbs

By 1970 pressure for the closure of the Alton line was mounting too, and this time the opposition was more organised against the threat. It was to culminate in a noisy public meeting at which all sorts of allegations were made, the main feature of which being the timing of the last BR census; mid week in August. Ironically too there were those, including at least one very high ranking official, on the railway who believed the line should be retained for its use as a diversionary route. They pointed out that over-estimation of materials required for the main line electrification had resulted in sufficient being left over to equip the branch at almost no extra cost. It was then left to the Secretary of State to reach a conclusion and subsequently he announced as being in favour of closure as soon as suitable alternative bus services could be provided.

This was finally arranged and amidst a flurry of flash bulbs and well wishers, the Mid Hants line passed into the annals of history one dark February night in 1973.

Locally it was hoped that the newly formed Mid Hants Railway Preservation Society could take over the running of the line complete, possibly with a service between Alton and Winchester, or at least as far as Springvale, where a halt would be built and a bus service to connect with the main line station. Sadly this failed for a variety of reasons and the society instead concentrated on the preservation of the Alresford–Alton section as a tourist line.

The withdrawal of the Alton trains meant that the line from Winchester to Southampton was served by two less trains hourly, a situation not appreciated by many travellers. Alternative arrangements were made to a degree with the rerouting of the Reading–Salisbury diesel service to a Reading–Portsmouth service via Eastleigh, some such services remaining to the present time.

Into the 80s

Meanwhile BR had at last realised the value of the motor car in so far as parking was concerned, large areas of waste land being opened up as station car parks including the former goods yard at Winchester station. Ironically the revenue from this meant that parking charges almost equalled, if not exceeded, former goods receipts, a situation impossible to contemplate a few short decades ago.

With the opening in 1985 of the M3 throughout between Sunbury near London to Winchester a new challenge faced the railway, and for the first time the valuable commuter traffic is at great risk. It will be interesting to observe the railways response to this. As this book goes to press, new rolling stock is being delivered and electrification is being extended to Weymouth. This will certainly help the route's competitive position. But even if there now exists just one line compared with three there is always the prospect of expansion; the recent oil find near South Wonston north of Worthy Down provides the possibility of a revival of the railway from Winchester Junction as far as Worthy Down where a loading point could be established. Certainly it would make sense rather than submit the roads to extra tanker traffic or decimate the countryside for a pipeline, especially when the trackbed is still present. Perhaps one day the true value of the railway will be recognised, instead of having to prove pounds and pence on a balance sheet in Whitehall.

A strange formation consisting of a class 73 electric on each end (73142 *Broadlands* and 73139) with 4 TC unit 8029 and temporary 4 TCB unit 2804 sandwiched in-between on the one hour late 13.44 Waterloo–Bournemouth on 25th July 1987. By the time this book appears, trains with class 73s on each end will have become commonplace due to late delivery and technical problems with the new class 442 units.

Chris Wilson

The shape of things to come. The new class 442 five-car electric multiple units are to take over all express services between Waterloo and Weymouth. Here unit No. 2403, viewed from Andover Road Bridge, runs past the former goods yard at Winchester on a crew training run to London from Bournemouth depot. *David C. Warwick*

ACKNOWLEDGEMENTS

Any non fiction book must out of necessity rely heavily upon the goodwill and kindness of others; the present work is no exception. Accordingly we would like to express our gratitude to all those who have so willingly assisted us in this way, our old friends especially but also those we have been privileged to meet for the first time.

In alphabetical order our thanks to:

Richard Avery, Eric Best, Ian Best, Bernard Briggs, Mrs Capon, Derek Clayton, Derek Dine, Roger Elsom, Les Elsey, John Fairman, Janet Grant, Graham and Betty Hawkins, Bob Irwin, Tony Molyneaux, Richard Nash, Alack Osman, Reg Randall, Dick Riley, Ian Shawyer, Malcolm Snellgrove, Ivor Snook, Peter Squibb, Paul Stock, Phillipa Stevens, Dennis Tillman, Arthur Watts and Chris Webb.

Also all those whose photographs have been used and anyone else we have inadvertently omitted from the credits. The following organisations have also been consulted:

Hampshire County Library, Hampshire County Record Office, The Public Record Office, British Rail, Southern and Western Regions.

Once again thanks to our long suffering wives, Lyn and Linda, perhaps we had better keep quiet about their involvement.

Finally the following books and periodicals have been consulted:

The Southern Railway Magazine & Great Western Railway Magazine (various issues), The Didcot, Newbury & Southampton Railway by Karau, Parsons & Robertson and the supplement to the above by Robertson & Simmonds.